The Good Cat Spell Book

About the Author

Gillian Kemp is an internationally acclaimed author of books about magic. Her best-known work, *The Good Spell Book,* topped the official UK book sales chart and was a huge success in the US, Canada, and Australasia. It was translated in Japan and across Europe.

Gillian has first-hand experience of the effectiveness of her spells for she regularly uses them to help family and friends. She has received many letters from her readers to tell her they have used her spells successfully, and to thank her for the accuracy of her predictions.

See more about Gillian at GillianKemp.com.

The Good Cat Spell Book

GILLIAN KEMP

Chicago, Illinois

The Good Cat Spell Book © 2025 by Gillian Kemp. All rights reserved. No part of this book may be reproduced in any manner whatsoever without written permission from Crossed Crow Books, except in the case of brief quotations embodied in critical articles and reviews.

Paperback ISBN: 978-1-959883-97-5
Library of Congress Control Number on file.

Disclaimer: Crossed Crow Books, LLC does not participate in, endorse, or have any authority or responsibility concerning private business transactions between our authors and the public. Any internet references contained in this work were found to be valid during the time of publication, however, the publisher cannot guarantee that a specific reference will continue to be maintained. This book's material is not intended to diagnose, treat, cure, or prevent any disease, disorder, ailment, or any physical or psychological condition. The author, publisher, and its associates shall not be held liable for the reader's choices when approaching this book's material. The views and opinions expressed within this book are those of the author alone and do not necessarily reflect the views and opinions of the publisher.

Published by:
Crossed Crow Books, LLC
6934 N Glenwood Ave, Suite C
Chicago, IL 60626
www.crossedcrowbooks.com

Printed in China.
APO

Other Books by the Author

The Good Dog Spell Book (Crossed Crow Books, 2025)
Spirits in Flowers Oracle Deck (CICO Books, 2025)
Celtic Goddesses and Their Spells (Ryland Peters & Small, 2023)
The Celtic Goddess Oracle Deck (CICO Books, 2022)
Tree Magick (CICO Books, 2022)
The Good Spell Book (Little, Brown, 2021)
The Modern Wiccan Box of Spells (CICO Books, 2018)
Mermaids and Dolphins and Magical Creatures of the Sea (CICO Books, 2007)
Faerie Wisdom Oracle (CICO Books, 2003)
The Love Magic Book (Little, Brown, 2003)
Good Witch Bad Witch Spell Box (Bulfinch, 2002)
The Dream Book (Little, Brown, 2001)
The Love Spell Box (Bulfinch, 2000)
The Fortune-Telling Book (Little, Brown, 2000)
The Love Spell Book (Orion Publishing Group, 2003)
Tea, Leaves, Herbs, and Flowers (Element Children's Books, 1998)

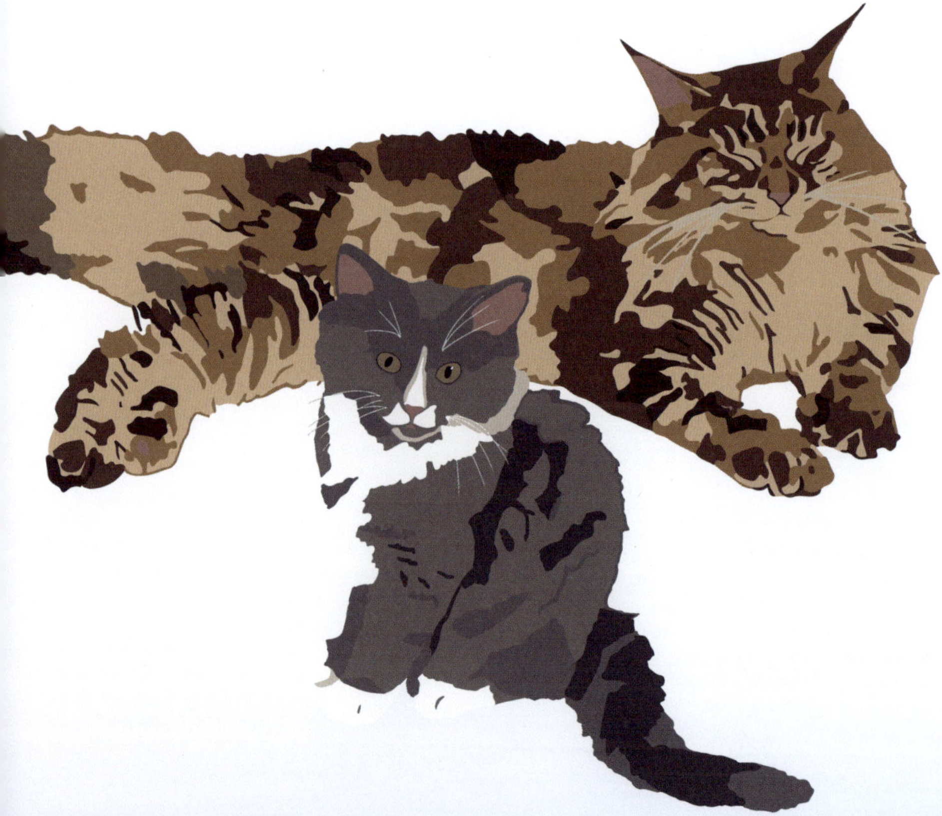

Contents

1. The Cat as Your Familiar — 1
2. Cats as Objects of Worship and Fear — 7
3. Spells for Love and Romance — 15
4. Spells for Happiness and Luck — 31
5. Spells for Wealth and Good Fortune — 43
6. Spells for Health and Healing — 55
7. Felidomancy: Feline Divination — 67
8. Know Your Cat by Their Astrological Sign — 81
9. Using the Good Cat Oracle — 109

Index — 131

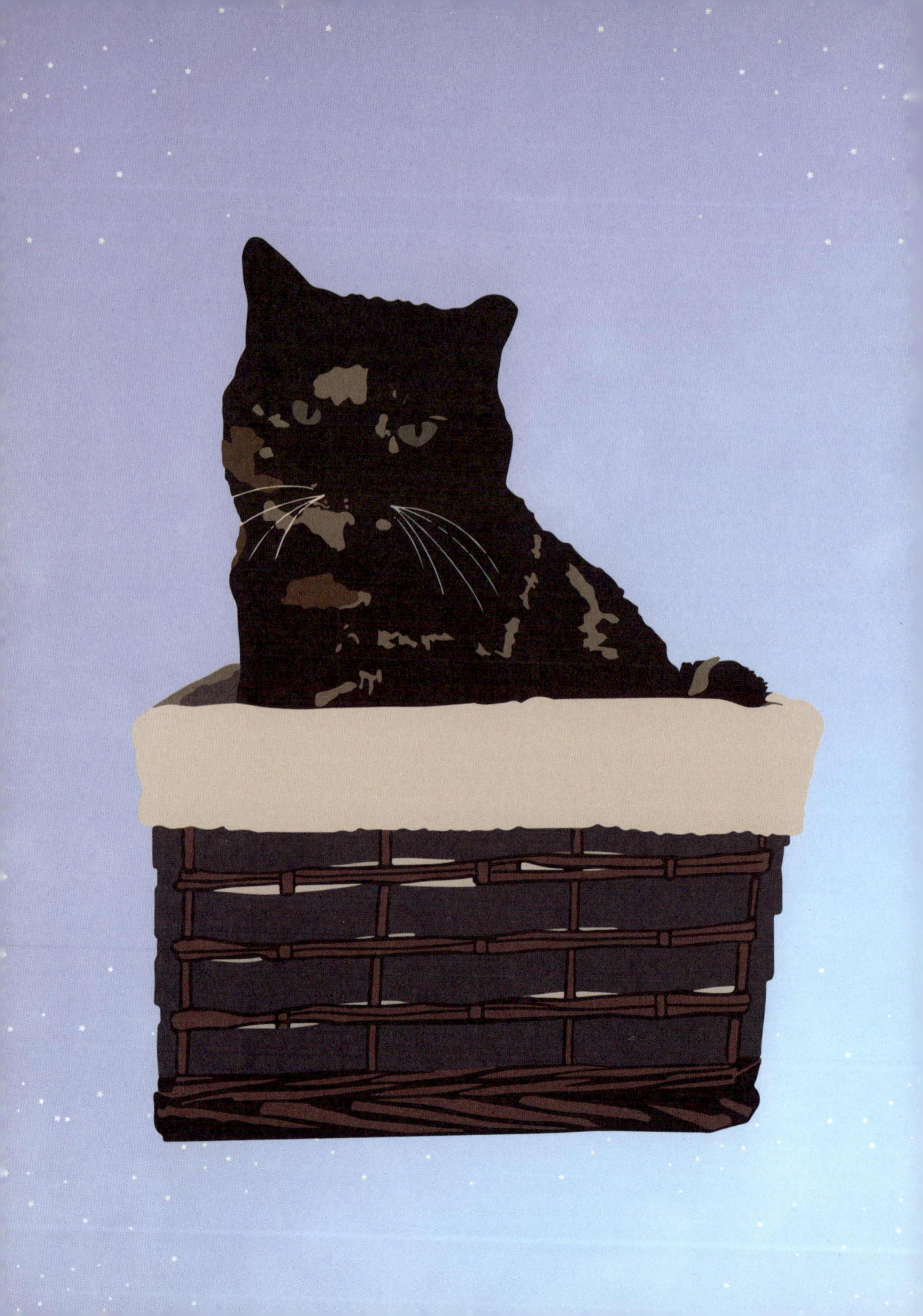

Chapter One

The Cat as Your Familiar

*C*ats are believed to possess the power to bewitch people. But people can bewitch cats, too. Call to a cat and, more often than not, they will approach you.

The magic has already begun if a cat has wandered into your life and adopted you as their owner. That cat has already bewitched you, and it is your duty to respect, look after, and love them.

A *familiar* is an animal companion who helps their person in their magical work. Your cat, then, is your familiar because the pair of you love each other. You know your cat loves you when they follow you around the house, insist on sleeping on your bed, and shadow your every move.

Your cat identifies your different tones of voice and responds to you with unique meows, purrs, and mannerisms. The love you and your cat share is a psychic and magical bond that creates profound, loving power, enhancing your magic and increasing the potency of your spells. The stronger the love link between you and your cat, the stronger your spells will be. As your familiar, bound to you by enduring love, your cat delivers your wishes. You and your cat's patience and respect for each other will channel and release magic.

Your cat must trust you and feel safe and secure in your love. Love is the connection to the spiritual realm where your spells are activated, because this is where you connect to the light of the universe and the source of all life. The bond of love cannot be broken—not even by death.

Naturally possessing intuitive insight, your cat probably knows and understands you better than any human. If your cat is your familiar, you will create an interdependence with them, in which neither of you is complete without the other because your lives are inextricably intertwined. Cats of any sex symbolize the abundant, maternal essence we call upon for help.

Cats' eyes represent the clairvoyant eyes of inner intuition, through which we see the truth to discover ourselves and our place in the world. If you look into their eyes, you will see the true, clear sight of omniscience, the seed of divine all-knowing. Look into your cat's eyes and you will have a window into the psychic world.

Cats see in the dark what a human cannot. Bast, the cat-headed goddess who presided over ancient Egyptian temples, represented the threshold of enlightenment where the conscious and unconscious minds met and blended. Whether you believe in spells or not, you can invoke the powers of Bast to help protect your familiar from harm and to bring your cat a long, happy, and healthy life in your care.

Magic is your inner power to direct events. Focusing your thoughts on what you want and wish and hope for is what brings results. The more people who direct their thoughts toward the same wish, the more powerful the spell, because their minds are channeled in the same direction. It is the same when you are working with your cat. They can add natural potency to your spells because of the emotional and psychic connections you share. Your faith in your spell also has an impact on its efficacy. Belief brings positive results in spellcasting.

Facing east when spellcasting gives extra vitality and power because the Sun rises in the east. If you have a garden where your cat has a favorite place to relax and you feel good, you can connect more directly with the elements and life-force energies. Every part of nature, including animals, trees, plants, and the weather, is an occult link to wish fulfillment. Spells for love, happiness, wealth, and health enlist the forces of nature.

Light is the energy of God and the universe. Nothing in nature can live without it. Light is also warmth, which is essential for life. When you light a candle, you link into Heaven's will and blessing by evoking the power of light. The thought or spoken words you put into lighting the candle continue to ascend to the heavenly or higher light for as long as the candle continues to burn. It is the same with incense.

Your cat will help you to do your magical work in a variety of ways, offering guidance as well as magical tools. For thousands of years, their actions have been interpreted as omens and the things they have discarded from their own bodies have been used for magic. For some spells, you'll need whiskers, milk teeth, fur, and claws that your cat has shed. Store them in a small "cat magic" trinket box until you require them for sorcery.

Your familiar may be trying to tell you something through their behavior, giving you cues you can follow to enhance your magic. For instance, cats love digging their claws into carpeting and furniture for fun. When they do this, wish for something that you would like to have within your grasp. They also like the warmest spot in the best seat in the house, so wish for something or someone to warm toward you when

The Good Cat Spell Book

your familiar takes your chair. And when your familiar sits on your lap, listen telepathically to what they are saying to you. Paying attention to your cat will develop your intuition and psychic abilities.

When you extend your finger to your cat and they cling to it with their velvety paws, wish for something or someone you want to cling to you. Silently, your cat may be telling you to grasp a situation and hold on to someone or something coming your way.

When your cat is lazing in a sunbeam, they may be trying to get your attention to tell you something or someone sunny is about to enter your life, bringing light and happiness to you. Wish it if you want it. And when your cat's eyes shine like lanterns, your familiar may be telling you that you are blessed by Heaven or that something good is about to happen for you. Ask for the light in your cat's eyes to shine on you and for the eternal light of love in your soul to keep burning brightly.

Your cat is your friend for life, sharing your working hours and solitary moments. Your familiar seems to know weekdays from weekends, too. Cats appear to have a built-in clock that makes them lick your face, nuzzle you with their nose, or walk around your head with small bunting, touching, and leaning gestures a little before the alarm clock is set to go off. They know a lot about relaxation, comfort, and sleep. Cats are peaceful to have around.

When you cast your spells, do not be put off if your cat gives you one of their snooty looks, as if to say, "I don't think much of you, you must be mad," and starts licking their paws and washing their face. Connect to your cat's behavior; your cat speaks without words. Allow your familiar to guide you on their magical path and let them work their age-old cat magic on you.

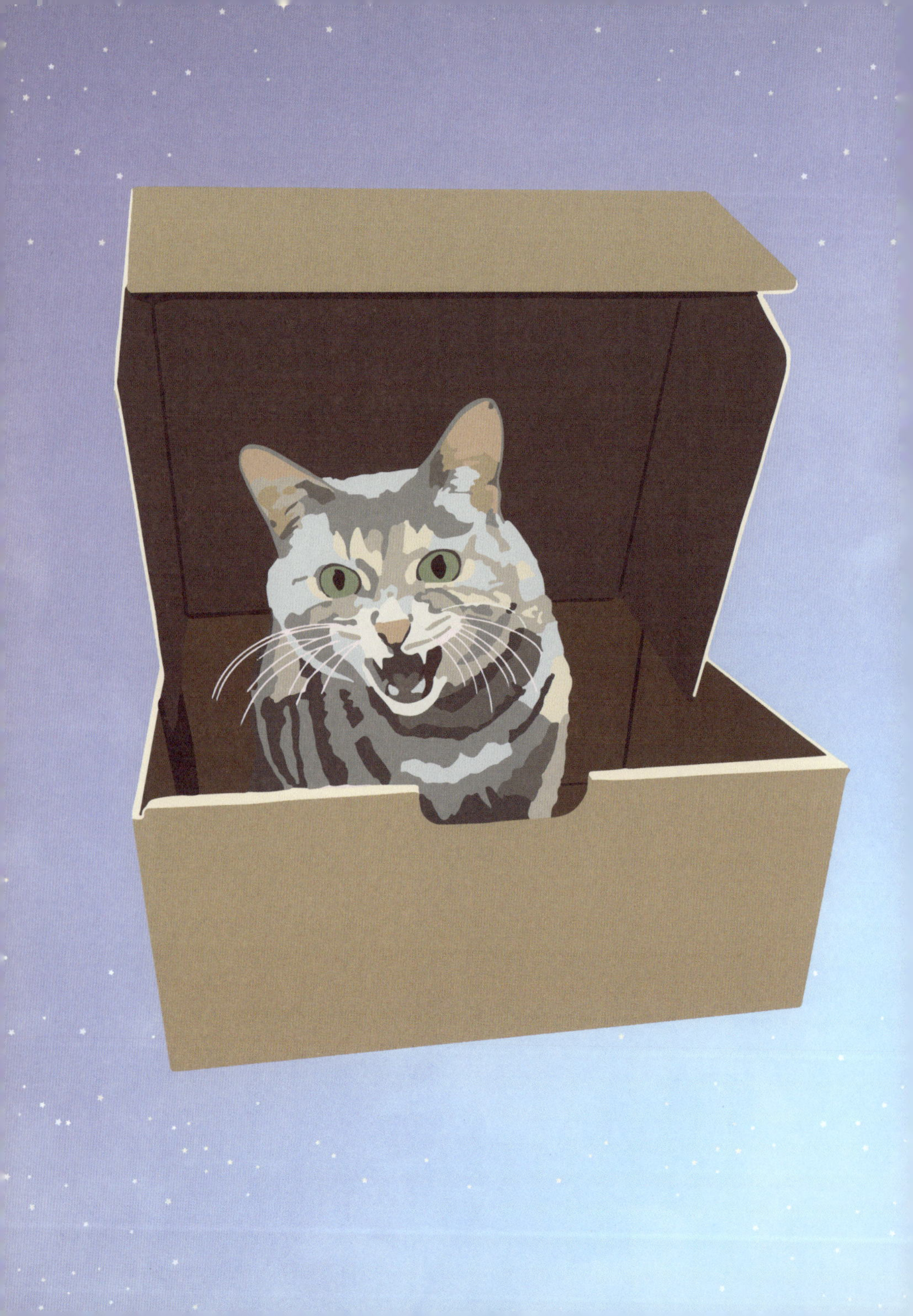

Chapter Two

Cats as Objects of Worship and Fear

$\mathcal{C}$ats gained their magical reputation for many reasons in different eras. They are creatures of the night, their meow is unearthly, and they love to sleep all day. Their pupils alter from a narrow vertical line by day to a luminous globe like the full moon at night. A cat luckily dupes fate by always landing on their feet. Their eyes follow things they appear to see that are invisible to us. Cats also seem to turn up from nowhere, take to us, and adopt us as their keeper. They have a mystery all their own.

The word *cat* occurs in numerous languages. Ireland, Lithuania, Afghanistan, and Sweden all have old words that sound like "puss" to refer to cats, and the words seem to come from the sound cats make.

Ancient Egypt had an exceptional fondness and reverence for cats; the cat-headed goddess Bast was worshipped by the Egyptians thousands of years ago. Egyptian figures and paintings of the period show cats wearing earrings and jeweled collars, and thousands of mummified cats have been found in tombs and buried along the Nile. So revered were cats in ancient Egypt that family members would shave off their eyebrows as a respectful sign of mourning and as sympathetic magic when their cat died. Killing a cat was a crime that carried the death sentence.

It may have been that every home had a cat for the simple reason that cats keep out mice. A home without a cat was not "homely." The cat was found in the center of Bubastis, in the center of Rome, and in the center of the family, guarding the hearth. The original domestication of cats is lost in antiquity, but it is believed the cat originally made its way from Libya into Egypt.

The ancient Egyptians regarded the cat as the "flaming eye of the Sun," Lady of Life, the soul of Osiris, and the eye of Ra, the Sun god. The Egyptians believed that when the Sun sank below the horizon every night, cosmic combat took place between Ra, the god of light, and Apep, the serpent of darkness. The cat was symbolic of the creative powers of the Sun, which rose every morning, having destroyed Apep. But Apep, being immortal, reappeared every night. And so the Cat's Cradle, a string game, was invented as sympathetic magic to control the movements of the Sun on which their lives depended. The game is still played today by children worldwide.

Bast, the goddess worshipped by the ancient Egyptians, sometimes had the complete body of a cat, but sometimes the head of a cat and body of a human dressed in embroidered garments. At the height of her power, Bast was revered as patroness of the eastern part of Nile delta, in the region called Tell-Basta in Bubastis. An amulet found there bears a message that reads: "May Bastet give life and power." The cat was thought to be a symbol of eternity and immortality because of the way it curls its tail around its head to form a circle. It was also believed to have nine lives thanks to its agility and tenacity. The number nine has long been believed to be lucky because it is a trinity of trinities. In Egyptian astronomy, there were nine spheres, and the Egyptian pantheon had nine gods. Nine was also significant to the Greeks: Apollo—brother of the Moon goddess Artemis—created a nine-month lunar year. And in Christianity, it is believed that Jesus died at the ninth hour.

The Egyptians and the Greeks associated the cat with the Moon as well as the Sun. Bast's parents were Moon deities, and her son Khensu was a Moon god. Her father was Horus, the sky god. Demetrius of Phalerum, a Greek poet, wrote that the size of a cat's body increased as the Moon grew from new to full and decreased as the Moon waned. Sometimes, the cat's eyes changing from crescent to round were likened to lunar phases. A cat's behavior, often becoming more active after sunset, is associated with the Moon. Even Irish poet William Butler Yeats wrote in his poem "The Cat and the Moon":

> *The cat went here and there*
> *And the moon spun round like a top*
> *And the nearest kin of the moon*
> *The creeping cat looked up.*

The cat cult of ancient Egypt continued well into the Roman period. The Romans called the cat *cattus,* the origin of the word "cautious." After the demise of cat worship in Egypt, similar practices sprang up in India, China, and Japan, and "cat clans" emerged in Teutonic, Celtic, and other lands. Pictures of Freya, the Norse goddess, show her chariot drawn by two cats.

By medieval times, cats were feared instead of worshipped. Cats' nocturnal instincts, intelligence, luminous eyes, unearthly cries, and the static electricity of their fur earned them the reputation of possessing demonic powers. So cats suffered persecution, along with the people who owned or befriended cats.

An epidemic of witch persecution raged in the fifteenth, sixteenth, and seventeenth centuries in Europe. Witches were believed to be in sympathy with the devil, whom they supposedly met at nighttime sabbats to concoct mischief and devilment. To attend a sabbat, it was believed a witch would anoint their feet and shoulders with the fat of a murdered baby, then mount a broomstick and exit the household chimney into the nighttime sky.

From 1450 to 1750, no one, including nuns and monks, was safe from being accused of witchcraft. Not attending church was a sign, and talking to your cat was another. Many people were condemned as witches simply because they kept household cats.

Witchcraft paranoia arrived in Britain in 1563 and even spread to Salem, in the Massachusetts colony, in 1692. Two women were executed for witchcraft in Northampton, England, as late as 1705.

Jane Wenham, the last person to be tried for witchcraft in Britain in 1712, was accused and found guilty at the Hertford Assizes of "conversing familiarly with the devil in the form of a cat." But she was pardoned and lived until 1730.

Many witches were convicted for sending a "wantounne cat" to avenge people. They were also accused of having "carriers": cats who stole milk, cream, cheese, and meat to be feasted on at sabbats. A black cat being called a witch's "familiar" originates from a medieval superstition that the devil's favorite form to take was that of a black cat. At the beginning of the fourteenth century, when Pope Clement V overthrew the Knights Templars, some tortured members of the order confessed to worshipping the devil in the form of a black tomcat.

In England, however, the white cat was considered unlucky because white made them visible to their prey. But since white cats often have one eye a different color from the other, they have always been considered magical and more capable than any other cat to predict good fortune. If your familiar is a white cat, it is believed you will have exceedingly good fortune your whole life long. Within twelve months of acquiring your white cat, someone in your close family will marry.

A deaf white cat with blue eyes is said to be especially psychic because their impeded hearing is directed inward to their inner ear, the psychic center. And blue-eyed cats of any color are said to be especially magical because, like blue sky over nighttime darkness, they symbolize divine eternity and immortality.

Folk beliefs about cats have persisted into modern times. In nineteenth-century England, sailors' wives liked to have a black cat as a pet. They were well-fed on fish in the belief that the black cat could and would charm safety into the lives of the women's husbands at sea. For further good luck, some wives sent their husbands off to sea with a little black fur cut from the cat's coat. In the fishing communities, it was considered lucky if a black cat ran toward a fisherman, and a sign of a bad catch if the cat crossed the fisherman's path to their ship or boat. Because black cats were considered lucky, they were frequently stolen.

The spells in the following chapters draw on cat wisdom that has survived the test of time. All are offered in the spirit of doing good, never doing harm.

Lucky Cats

According to age-old tradition, it is a lucky sign when a black cat crosses your path.

It's an old saying: "When you are walking along the street, it is a lucky sign a black cat to meet." Other lucky cat omens include:

- **It is lucky to be visited by a black cat and unlucky to shoo a black cat away.**
- **To dream of a black cat is a premonition of good luck, happy news, or a delightful event.**
- **To possess a black cat who grows one white hair is a sign of luck in love and affairs of the heart.**
- **If you see a black cat, stroke it three times and make a wish. Your wish will come true.**
- **Buddhists believe that light-colored cats ensure a wealth of silver, and dark-colored cats ensure a wealth of gold.**
- **If a tabby or gray cat wanders into your home, it is an omen of money.**
- **To own a tortoiseshell cat is a sign that you will always be lucky.**
- **It is a lucky omen if a cat wanders into your home and adopts you.**
- **Cats with double claws are thought to bring luck to their owners.**
- **A cat acquired in the month of May is said to be a cat more likely to catch birds and snakes than rodents.**

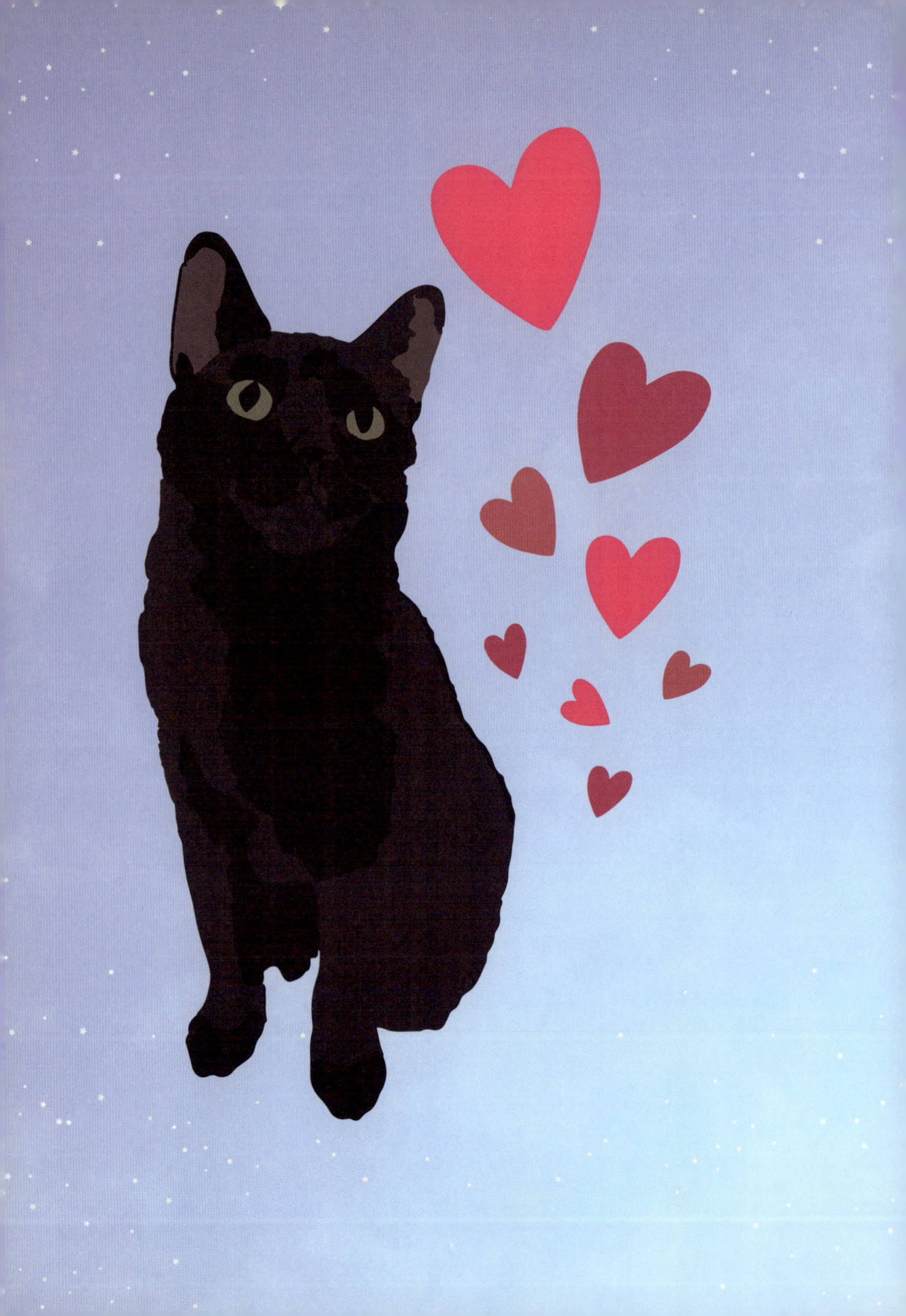

Chapter Three

Spells for Love and Romance

Love is everybody's favorite feeling, including your cat's. Your cat is a strong love-link who carries the wisdom of the nature of the higher world because they live in the etheric plane—that is, in a subtle form of energy on a higher plane than matter. It is in the ether that the elements of Air, Fire, Water, and Earth are put into action and take effect to become matter. The ether comes from the origin of the universe, which is love.

Your cat has supernatural ability to see the unseen, and by harmonizing with their love frequency, you connect through them to the love wave in the ether so that it runs through you and carries you along to where you want to be. The love frequency flows through every living part of nature. By aligning yourself to the supernatural forces, you can direct love to you, because the supernatural forces are ruled by love and are sympathetic to your inner resonance.

Friday, ruled by the love planet Venus, is the most potent day of the week for casting love spells. In general, it is best to perform spells to bring love to you while the Moon is waxing (becoming full), and spells to drive unrequited love away while the Moon is waning.

To Bewitch the One You Love

This is a good springtime spell to perform when love is in the air and your feline friend is shedding and feeling frisky.

You will need:
- **1 pink candle**
- **1 blue candle**
- **Fur from your cat's brush**
- **Clean white paper**
- **A pen or pencil**
- **A saucer**
- **Milk or water**

Brush your cat or stroke their fur. Remove the fur from the brush or your fingers and place it on an unused piece of white paper.

With your cat present, light the pink candle to represent yourself and the blue candle to represent the one you love.

Write your name on a small piece of white paper and the name of the one you desire beneath yours. Sprinkle cat fur over your names and fold the paper into a small envelope to contain the fur. Burn the paper in both flames while saying:

> *"As fur burns in this flame,*
> *Into your mind enters my name.*
> *As your name burns,*
> *To me your heart turns.*
>
> *During my cat's nocturnal hours,*
> *(Name of cat) will work on you their magical powers.*
> *I will be in your dreams while you rest,*
> *Until you grant my love request."*

Place the paper in the saucer to reduce it to ashes and play with your cat while the candles burn. Tell them you know they will help you to win the heart of the one you desire. Snuff the candles out. Bury the ash. Wash the saucer and pour some milk or water into it for your cat to drink.

To Draw Romance to You

You will need:
- **1 pink-colored or rose-scented candle**
- **Lavender-scented incense**
- **A little cat fur**

Light the candle and the lavender incense, and make sure that both are safe. Switch off all electric lighting and lie down with your cat's heart across your heart. Stroke your cat until they purr. Breathe in synchronous rhythm with the purring to slow the mind, creating alpha brain waves that connect you to the ether where all knowledge is.

Tell your cat that you are asking, with their help, for the light of the candle flame to bring a perfect partner into your life. Then say:

*"Cat be nimble,
Cat be quick.
As the flame burns the wick,
Bring me true love quick."*

If you see or feel static electricity when your cat is on your heart and you are stroking them, it reveals that you have created a magic spark of attraction, perhaps in the life of someone whom you have already met. Do not try to create static, but take it as a good sign if it occurs naturally.

After relaxing as long as you like with your cat, sprinkle a little fur that may already be on your hands or picked up from your clothes into the candle flame. Then, snuff out the candle.

To Attract a New Lover

Friday night would be the most potent time to cast this love spell.

You will need:
- **1 pink or red candle**
- **Rose oil**
- **A straight pin**

Stroke your cat with your fingertips and anoint the top half of the candle with rose oil, from the top to the center, to attract love toward you and your cat. Using the pin, write on the candle the name of the one you desire. As you light the candle, say:

"This flame of love will ignite flames of passion that burn within the heart of (name of person). (She/He/They) will love me."

At midnight, snuff out the candle, saying:

"My wish is sealed by the witching hour."

Take your cat to bed with you to seal the spell. Wait in the patience of time, and the one you have bewitched will contact you. Alternatively, your paths will cross as if by coincidence.

You will have a male visitor if your cat washes their face with their right paw over their right ear. If they wash their face and left ear with their left paw, expect a female visitor.

To Keep the One You Love

The new moon is the best time for this spell.

You will need:
- **1 silver candle**
- **Your cat's brush**
- **A handkerchief or scrap of fabric**
- **Red cotton thread**
- **A needle**

Settle your cat beside you and light the silver candle at the time of a new moon. Brush your cat's fur and remove the shed fur from the brush. On a handkerchief or scrap of fabric, use red cotton thread to stitch the first name and surname of the one you desire in running stitch, inserting strands of fur to secure them by the thread as you stitch.

Sleep with the handkerchief under your pillow, and the one you love will be true to you. If you decide you want to walk away from the relationship, undo the stitching and burn or bury the handkerchief, thread, and fur.

To Encourage a Lover's Feelings to Grow

You can make love grow especially well if you start this spell at the new moon. Catmint (*Nepeta faassenii*) is governed by the love planet Venus.

You will need:
- **A garden, or potting compost and an indoor pot**
- **A catmint plant**

Dig a hole in your garden or place some potting compost in an indoor pot and push a catmint plant into the soil. Ask your cat to make paw prints in the soil. As the catmint grows, so too will love for you grow in the heart of the one you desire.

To Encourage a Long-Time Love to Endure

Start this spell when the Moon is waxing. As a symbol of the soul and life, salt can be used as a charm to perpetuate a relationship.

You will need:
- **1 pink candle**
- **An unused envelope**
- **Salt**

During the waxing phase of the Moon, drop a pinch of salt into an envelope and place it in or beneath your cat's bed so that they will sleep on it.

When the Moon is full, light a pink candle and slowly sprinkle the salt into the candle flame. As the flame burns blue, say:

> *"When the Moon is round,*
> *Good luck will abound.*
> *Seek and you shall find,*
> *What is now within your mind.*
> *Your thoughts shall always turn to me,*
> *You and I will always be we."*

Snuff out the candle. Roll the envelope into a ball shape and roll it across the floor so that your cat chases it, symbolizing the way the one you love will chase you.

To Attract Your Soulmate

When measuring your cat's shadow, make sure the sunlight is behind you so that the shadow is in front.

You will need:
- **A long ruler or measuring tape**
- **Lipstick**
- **A pen with green ink**
- **A small piece of red, pink, or green paper**

Spells for Love and Romance

When your cat is stretching, perhaps to sharpen their claws, or curled up basking in sunlight, measure their shadow from nose to tail.

Put lipstick on your cat's right front paw. To take your cat's paw print, encourage them to step onto the small piece of colored paper, stand them on the colored paper, or press the piece of colored paper to their paw. Beside the paw print, measure and record the length of the shadow. Fold the paper to conceal the paw print and the number.

Put the piece of paper inside your right shoe. When you go outside, say in your mind to the rhythm of your walk:

> *"I will attract my soul mate,*
> *And be asked for a date.*
> *Like cat love I wear in my shoe,*
> *True love come to me to woo."*

You will find that you will attract a partner. When you do, be discerning and question yourself about whether the person is right for you.

Symbolically, cats are the guardians of marriage. That is why in England, brides sometimes carried a black cat along with their wedding bouquet.

To Persuade an Unwanted Suitor to Retreat

Do this spell during a waning moon.

You will need:
- **An unused envelope**
- **Salt**
- **Access to a running stream, river, or the sea**

Place an unused envelope containing three pinches of salt in your cat's basket, under their bed, or wherever they will happily sleep on the sealed envelope for a few nights. By being in close contact, the salt will be influenced by your cat's feelings.

Take the envelope of salt to a running stream or a river, or to the sea when the tide is going out. Throw a pinch of salt into the water, saying:

"(Name of person), the tide has turned."

Throw in a second pinch, saying:

"You will flow out of my life."

Throw in a third pinch, saying:

"I have broken from you in my mind."

Sprinkle the remaining fragments of salt into the water and bury the envelope. Walk away without looking back to leave the past behind you. The person concerned will painlessly flow out of your life, as surely as streams flow to rivers and rivers flow to seas.

To Encourage an Unwanted Lover to Let Go

You will need:
- **2 straight pins**
- **1 blue candle**

Leave a blue candle in your cat's basket during a waxing moon. The feline powers they exude will be absorbed by the candle.

When the Moon becomes full, insert a pin through the candle from left to right so that it pierces the wick and appears through the wax on the opposite side. Cross the first pin as closely as possible with a second pin next to it, pressed through the wick from left to right. The pins should cross paths.

With your cat purring beside you, light the candle. Ring the bell on their collar, if they have one, to clear the air and to draw down power from Heaven to Earth.

As the candle burns through the pins, the lover you are redirecting will realize that the relationship is over. If the pins move around while the candle is burning, turn the candle to point the pin tips in the direction of your lover's home. The person will get the point and withdraw. The crossed pins provide a crossroad so the person can find other directions to take. Snuff out the candle after it has burned past the pins.

To End a Relationship

This type of spell is known as a banishing and is most effective when performed during the waning moon.

You will need:
- **1 white candle**
- **Milk or water**
- **A pen with black ink**
- **Clean white paper**

Pour enough milk or water into your cat's dish so that they drink but leave some. On an unused piece of white paper, write the name of your lover, whom you wish to leave you in peace. Beneath the name, write: *"Realize I do not want a relationship with you."*

Draw a thick black border around the words. Flick milk or water from your cat's bowl onto the paper. Leave the paper to dry.

With your cat settled and purring beside you, light a candle and burn the paper in its flame while saying:

*"By cat-bright eyes and candlelight,
Feline purrs chase vermin out of sight."*

The person on whom you have cast your spell will sense that you have detached yourself from them in your mind. They will either suddenly contact you to see whether they still have power over you or withdraw without resistance.

For a Lover to Return to You

You will need:
- **2 bay leaves**
- **2 paper clips**
- **1 red candle**
- **1 pink candle**
- **A ballpoint pen**
- **A little fur from your cat's brush**
- **An unused envelope or one that your lover has written your name upon**

Stroke your cat with both candles so that your cat's personality and personal magnetism rub off onto the candles.

Using the pen, write your name on the pink candle and your lover's name on the red candle. Place the candles in two holders set about seven inches apart. Light the candles and slide them slowly toward each other, so that the candleholders touch, while you say:

*"You are moving closer to me and returning
While these two candles are burning."*

Look into the flames, then close your eyes and visualize you and your lover laughing together.

Write your name on one bay leaf and your lover's name on another. Put a little cat fur on the bay leaf that bears your lover's name. Place the bay leaf with your name on top of the fur, sandwiching it in place. The names should face each other. Keep the bay leaves together with two paperclips. Put the leaves in an envelope, snuff out the candle, and sleep with the envelope under your pillow or inside your pillowcase. Your cat's static fur will draw your lover back to you.

A Magical Mirror Love Reflection Spell

You will need:
- **1 pink candle**
- **7 rose buds**
- **7 cloves**
- **A hand mirror or dressing table mirror**
- **A handkerchief or unused envelope**
- **About a six-inch length of pink ribbon**

Sit with your cat and stroke your cat until they purr, then hold a mirror to your cat's nose so that their breath makes the mirror foggy. Put your cat on your bed while you light the pink candle. Drop the rose buds and cloves into the center of a handkerchief and tie the cloth into a ball shape with the pink ribbon; alternatively, place them in the envelope and tie the ribbon around it.

Pick up your cat and sit so that you are both looking into the mirror, then say:

> *"Magic mirror in front of the wall,*
> *Attract one in true love with me to fall.*
> *May we bring out good in each other,*
> *And may they be a faithful lover."*

Continue to cuddle your cat before snuffing out the candle. Sleep with the tied handkerchief or envelope inside your pillowcase or carry the handkerchief or envelope close to your skin.

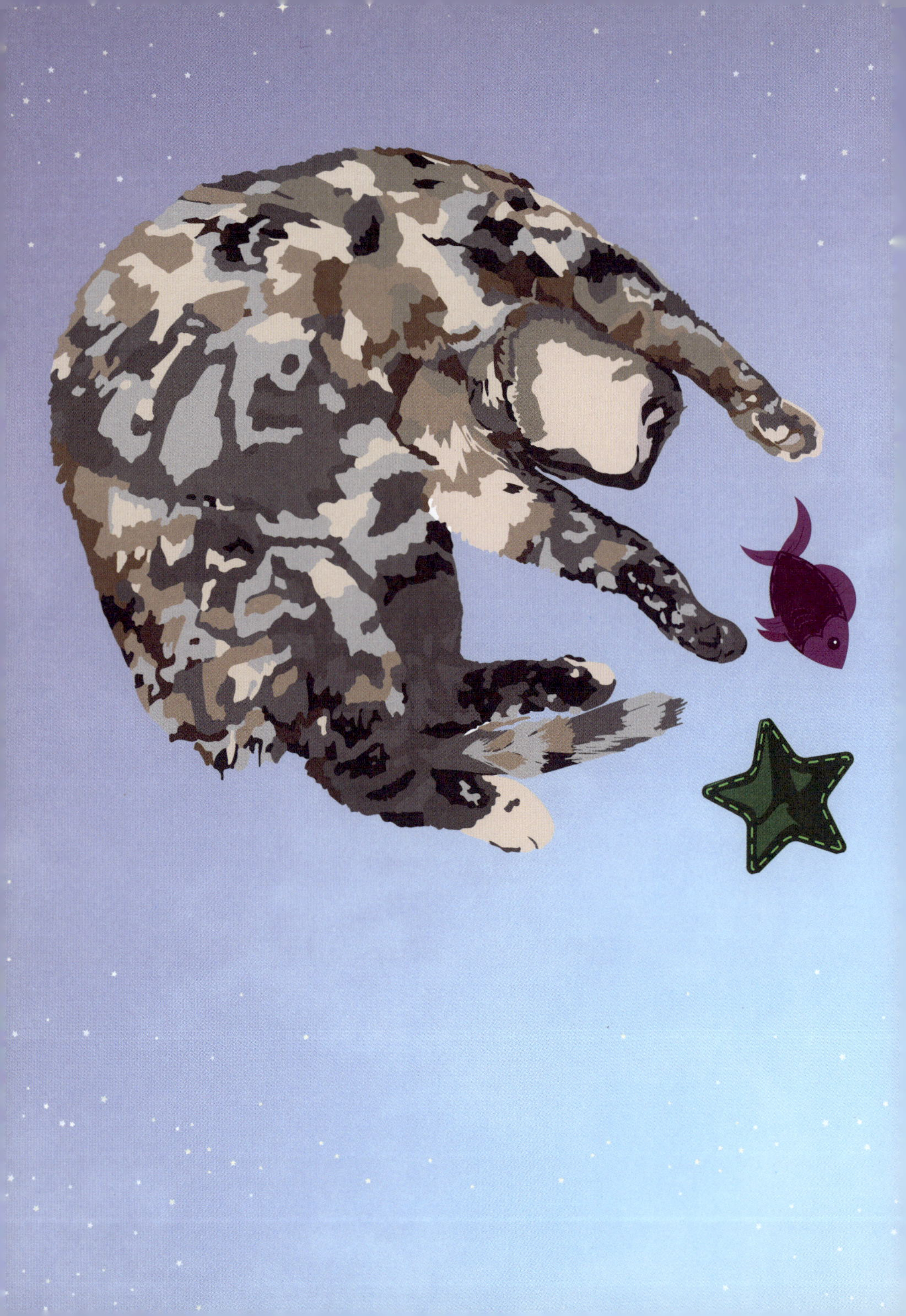

Chapter Four

Spells for Happiness and Luck

In life, do your best to be optimistic and try to be happy. Always keep a sense of humor. Follow your intuition, because it is your inner compass that points you in the right direction to do the right thing. The word *intuition* literally means "to be taught from within."

Relaxing with your cat helps you de-stress, and when you are calm like your cat, it is easier to tune in to your inner soul and essential nature.

To Transform Bad Luck to Good

The number eight symbolizes union.

You will need:
- **4 stalks of wheat, oats, or barley straw (soaked in water to make pliable)**
- **Thread or string**

Take the four stalks of straw and twist them in opposite directions in a figure eight. Tie the ends of the straw with thread.

Put the figure eight inside your cat's bed or basket and keep it there. Every time you see your cat jump out of or into their basket, say:

"Cat jump out, cat jump in,
Bad luck out and good luck in."

Alternatively, place the figure eight on the floor and play with your cat so that they jump on it or over it. It does not matter if the straw breaks.

When you no longer have use for the talisman, bury it or throw it in a stream, river, or the sea.

It is said to be lucky to have a cat living in a theater. It is an ill omen if a cat enters the stage during a performance, but to have a black cat in the audience on opening night is good luck.

To Make Something Special Happen

You will need:
- 1 candle
- A straight pin
- An acorn

Hold the candle in front of your cat so that your familiar scratches it with their paws. Using the pin, inscribe on the candle what it is you wish to happen. Then, insert the pin through the wick from right to left. Put the candle in the east on a table and light the candle while holding the acorn in your hand and saying:

> *"As the pin pierces the wick,*
> *It will work a magical trick.*
> *My inscription on the wax*
> *Will bring me (speak what it is that you want)."*

While still holding the acorn, sit with the candle until it burns through the pin and inscription. Snuff out the candle and bury the candle stub and pin in an eastern position outdoors.

For Good Weather on a Special Day

Cats dislike rain and can help drive it away. This spell requires no supplies. When your cat is sitting high or basking in a beam of sunlight, say:

*"(Day of the week) is my special day,
Kitty keep the rain away.
May you make the Sun shine,
May (day of the week) be fine."*

Look at a cloud in the sky and decide in your mind to bore a hole through the cloud to reveal blue sky or make the cloud move to the left or right. Stare at the cloud while you think it, and you will see for yourself that the cloud moves according to your command.

To Encourage Your Parents to Reconcile and Reunite

Sometimes feuding loved ones need a little help to get past their differences.

You will need:
- **Naturally shed cat fur**
- **Individual photos of both your parents**
- **A few paper clips**
- **A tiger's eye stone**

Place some cat fur between two photos of your parents. The photos should be positioned face-to-face and held together with paper clips. Place a tiger's eye stone on top of the photos and keep the photos with the stone on top among your personal possessions for as long as necessary.

If your cat cries, dashes around, and seems shocked for no apparent reason, they are telling you that a family argument is about to occur.

For Help to Pass a Test or Exam

The spirit world will help you to pass your exam as long as you do your bit by working and studying for it. On the day of the exam, say a prayer for the right answers to come into your mind. If you can't find a catnip plant (*Nepeta cataria*), use a catnip toy instead.

You will need:
- **Some catnip**
- **A handkerchief, scrap of cloth, or clean piece of paper**
- **A length of red ribbon or string**
- **An unused envelope (optional)**

Take a handful of catnip leaves. Hold them in your hand and you will find that the catnip warms up. Place the catnip on a handkerchief or piece of paper.

Hold your cat's paws in your hands while they are still warm. You will probably find that your cat tries to nuzzle their nose into your clasped hands, pushing them apart. At the moment you open your hands, say:

"I will pass my (subject) exam."

The Good Cat Spell Book

Tie the catnip into the handkerchief using the red ribbon or string, or place the paper with the catnip in an envelope and tie the ribbon around the envelope.

Place the handkerchief inside your pillowcase, and each night before going to sleep, say:

"I will pass my (name of) exam."

On the day of your exam, carry the catnip handkerchief with you. Afterward, give it to your cat to use as a toy.

For a Successful Job Interview

Basil is an herb that attracts wealth.

You will need:
- **A cat's whisker**
- **A basil plant in a pot or in the garden**
- **Lipstick**
- **A printed interview request**
- **A piece of unused paper**

When your cat is in your kitchen, show them the printed letter asking you to attend a job interview. Put lipstick on your cat's right front paw. Encourage your cat to walk onto the request to make a lipstick paw print, then another on a clean piece of paper. Bury the piece of paper in the basil plant's soil and insert your cat's whisker into the soil.

Use the basil in your cooking or eat a leaf every day before your job interview. The herb will nourish the bond you share with your cat and attract the job you are seeking. Carry the printed interview request in your purse, briefcase, or pocket to your job interview.

To Increase Your Popularity

The Egyptian ankh, a cross with a loop, represents eternal life.

You will need:
- **1 beetroot**
- **A fountain pen with a nib**
- **A clean piece of paper**

Place the beet in a pot with enough water to cover it and bring to a boil. Reduce the heat to low and simmer for about half an hour until it is soft. Leave it in the water to cool. Remove the beet, rub the skin, and eat the beet. Do not discard the cooking water.

Fill the fountain pen with the water in which you boiled the beet. On the clean piece of paper, write your name, followed by the names of people whom you already know and would like to see or be involved with more often. After their names, draw the sign of the ankh. Fold the paper to conceal the writing and the symbol.

While your familiar is resting, rub the piece of paper from the tip of their nose down their spine to the tip of their tail, then kiss your cat's nose while saying:

> *"This sign in Egyptian*
> *Is a prescription*
> *For me blending,*
> *Friendship unending."*

Bury the piece of paper in the soil of a potted plant or under a tree or garden plant. You will find that the people whose names you wrote will include you in their social lives.

To Bring Peace of Mind

No animal understands the healing power of sleep and relaxation better than the cat.

You will need:
- **A cat's whisker or some naturally shed fur**
- **A handkerchief or pouch**
- **Lavender flowers**
- **Chamomile flowers**
- **A short length of ribbon**

Put your cat's naturally shed whisker or fur into a handkerchief with lavender and chamomile flowers. Tie them in place and put the bundle inside your pillowcase; their scent will help you sleep.

When you lie in bed, close your eyes and tell your guardian angel what problem you would like solved. Say "thank you," knowing that you have already received what you are asking for.

You will find that the jigsaw pieces of your life start slotting into place, and have peace of mind knowing that you are able to call for help whenever you feel in need of assistance or comfort.

To Know Your Cat Is Happy While You Are Away

This spell works two ways: to bring joy to your holiday and to maintain your link to your cat while you are away.

You will need:
- **1 green, golden, or white candle**
- **A drop of milk in your cat's bowl**
- **A piece of paper with the name of your travel destination written on it**
- **A photograph of your cat**
- **An unused envelope**

Dip your cat's paw into the milk and press their paw onto the piece of paper you have written your holiday destination upon. Light the candle and hold the piece of paper at a safe distance above the candle flame to avoid lighting it on fire. The heat of the flame will turn the paw print brown.

Put the piece of paper and a photograph of your cat in the envelope and snuff out the candle. Put the envelope inside your suitcase or travel bag to take on holiday with you.

While away, look at the photograph of your cat and send love to them by thought.

To Keep Intruders Away

Your cat is territorial, so you can reinforce boundary lines with the help of your familiar. Garlic is ruled by the planet Mars, which protects from theft.

You will need:
- **1 head of garlic**
- **A pot of soil or a garden**
- **Some fur from your cat's brush**
- **A discarded whisker or claw sheath (if possible)**

Separate the cloves from the head of garlic. Take the pot of soil and bury some of your cat's fur, along with a discarded whisker or claw sheath if you have them. Break the head of garlic into individual cloves and peel the outer papery covering away. Press the cloves of garlic into the soil, ensuring the pointed side is up, and cover them with dirt.

Hold your cat and press one of their front paws into the soil to make one or more paw prints. Afterward, stroke your cat's whiskers and ears and say:

> *"I stroke your whiskers,*
> *And I stroke your ears.*
> *We have no fears.*
> *No intruder nears.*
> *All harmful people are kept away, at bay."*

The garlic cloves you have planted will multiply into heads of garlic, increasing the protective force around your home. If you potted the garlic cloves, keep the pot or pots beside your front or back door, inside or out, or alternatively on a windowsill that faces east (where the Sun rises).

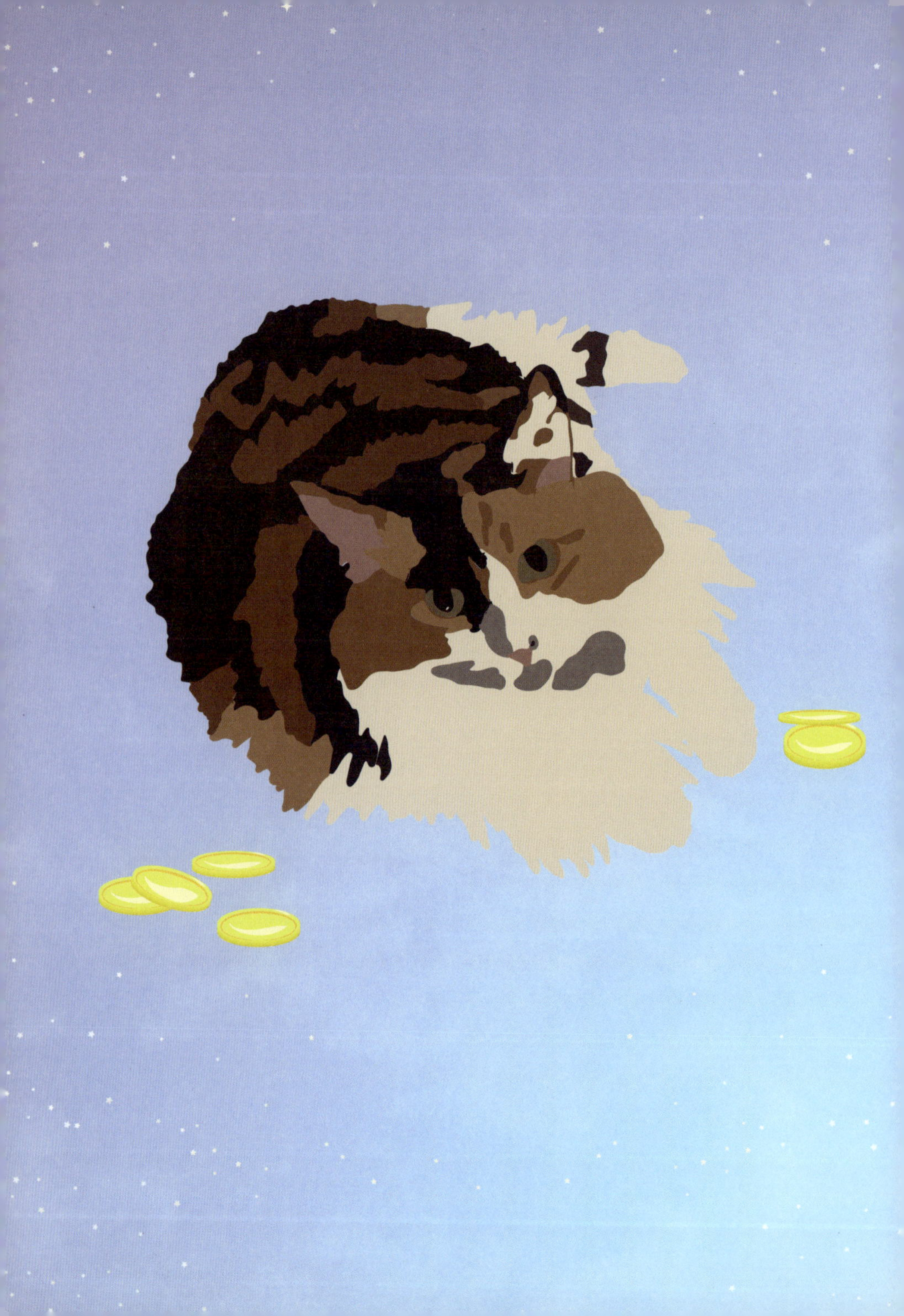

Chapter Five

Spells for Wealth and Good Fortune

There is nothing wrong with having money, except what you would do to get it and how you would use it once you have it. Mercury, the planet closest to the Sun, relates to gold and wealth, and for this reason, money spells often seek to tap into its energy. Often, money spells are performed on Wednesdays, the day of the week governed by Mercury. The fluid and dynamic character of Mercury has an unlimited capacity for transformation. Mercury also symbolizes your subconscious and will attract wealth to you because you need it. Because Mercury is the planet of wealth, if you link to its energy successfully, do not doubt that the money you need will arrive—sometimes immediately, other times not. The timing may also depend on whether we ourselves are at a high or low ebb. Sometimes we are more in sync with celestial forces and our own inner spiritual powers.

To Attract Money into Your Home and Life

This spell is particularly effective for attracting money to you quickly. It should be cast on a Wednesday. Because the waxing moon enhances growth in your life, cast your spell when the Moon is new, visible as a crescent in the sky with the horns pointing to the left.

You will need:
- **2 saucers or small dishes**
- **1 gold candle**
- **1 silver candle**
- **Fur from your cat's brush**
- **Loose change, uncounted**
- **Inside front doormat**
- **Cash (a high-value bill)**
- **Cat toy**
- **A pen**
- **Green paper**

Light the golden candle to represent the Sun and the silver candle to represent Mercury (the planet and elemental quicksilver).

Brush your cat while you tell them that you would like them to help bring money into your life as quickly as possible, not for greed but by necessity. Remove strands of their fur from the brush and place them in a saucer between the two candles. Put all your loose change in the saucer. Avoid calculating how much the coins add up to, because that would limit your expectations.

Take your cat to the doormat inside the main entrance of your home and let them see you place the bill under the doormat. Throw one of your cat's toys onto the doormat to entice them to leap there. Whatever money you place under the mat must be left there until a full moon, so deposit the largest amount you can afford.

With your cat beside you, sit in front of the candles and coins. On a piece of green paper, write everything you need the money for.

Burn the piece of paper by passing it first through the flame of the golden candle, then through the flame of the silver candle. Leave the paper to extinguish in a second saucer. Determine how many hours the candles should burn based on the number of money wishes you have. Every hour represents one wish. If you have three money wishes, let the candles burn in your presence for three hours before snuffing them out. You do not need to sit with the candles but need to be indoors. Gather the coins and return them to your purse, wallet, or wherever they were before you began casting your spell. Only remove the bill from under your doormat when the Moon is full or waning; otherwise, you may invite expense. If you can afford to, leave the bill indefinitely under the doormat. During the time the bill is under the mat, any visitor to your home will attract wealth to you by stepping on the doormat.

To Attract a Specific Amount of Money

This spell uses color symbolism to work its magic. Red is the color of blood, the life force; gold is the color of wealth and high spirituality.

You will need:
- **A piece of scrap paper**
- **A small piece of gold paper or a gold card**
- **A pen with red ink**
- **A photograph of your cat**

On the piece of scrap paper, write in capital letters the figure you need—for instance, "ten thousand dollars."

Delete all letters that are repeated in the words—in this case, T, N, O, S, A, D, and L. The letters that don't recur are H, E, U, and R (which sound rather like "here you are").

Write the letters H, E, U, and R in cursive script, with the letters attached, using red ink on a small piece of gold paper or a gold card. Place the card face-to-face with a picture of your cat in your purse or wallet. Keep it there to speed money to you.

When I cast this spell, I received the exact amount I asked for—two years later! I had forgotten about it until the gold paper came to my attention when I was transferring the contents of an old wallet to a new one.

To Speed Cash to You Quickly

You will need:
- **Some cash (any denomination, bills or coins)**
- **A roughly six-inch strand of gold-colored thread**
- **A jar or pot**
- **Catnip (optional)**

Put a pile of cash on the floor. Get your cat to rub their paws into it by sprinkling catnip over it. Alternatively, play with the coins to entice your cat to join in and touch the coins with their paws or body.

Roll the paper money into a cylinder and secure it with the gold thread. Keep the money scroll in your purse and do not spend it.

Put the pile of coins that you have sprinkled with catnip into a pot. Keep the pot in the eastern part of your home and do not spend the money. Because the east is where the Sun rises, every day you will attract new money into your home.

To Get Out of Debt

Cats and camphor don't mix; camphor is toxic to cats but not to you. Just to be extra cautious, it is probably best to keep your cat out of the kitchen when casting this spell.

This banishing spell must begin on the night the Moon is full.

You will need:
- **9 ice cubes**
- **9 new disposable cleaning cloths**
- **9 drops of camphor oil**
- **A dish**
- **Water from your cat's bowl**

On the night of a full moon, put nine ice cubes into a dish. Pour a little water from your cat's bowl over the ice. Sprinkle the ice with nine drops of camphor oil. When the ice has melted, go to where your cat is and tell them precisely what debt you would like them to help you clear. Without your cat following you into the kitchen, clean your stove by wiping the camphor and water solution with a brand-new cloth. Throw the cloth away afterward, wash your hands, and then play and talk with your cat.

Cast your spell again on the following eight consecutive nights. Keep your familiar out of the kitchen while melting the ice with camphor oil and cleaning the stove again. Each night, use a new cloth soaked in the water from the nine ice cubes melted with nine drops of camphor oil. The ice symbolically takes the heat out of the volatile situation represented by the camphor. The stove relates to your nourishment. If you cannot cast your spell on one of the nine nights, clean your stove during the day instead, but do not miss any twenty-four-hour period.

Before long, well-paid work, a windfall, or a check will arrive, enabling you to clear your debt. You may also find your debtor partially writing off the debt.

To Increase Your Wealth

Green represents wealth.

You will need:
- **A small piece of ginger root**
- **One of your cat's shed claws or a dressmaking pin**
- **A gold-colored coin**
- **A short length of green ribbon or thread**

Into the ginger root, insert a claw your cat has shed; alternatively, use a dressmaking pin. Bind the gold-colored coin to the ginger with green ribbon or thread. Keep the amulet in a secret place.

Three days before a full moon, put the amulet on a windowsill overnight, or carry it to a place where it is exposed to the Moon. Repeat this on the night before the full moon and on the night of the full moon. Then, return the amulet to its secret place.

By the time of the new moon (which always occurs two weeks after the full moon), you will find that your financial good fortune has increased.

To Sell Your Home for the Right Price

Before starting this spell, have a word with your cat and tell them that you want the right buyer to come along and offer you the price you want for the home that you or your family is selling.

You will need:
- **1 green candle**
- **A cat toy or short length of string**

With your familiar beside you, light the green candle. When your cat is in the mood to be picked up, carry them to one of the walls in the room. Dangle one of their toys or a piece of string against the wall so that your cat taps the wall with their paw. Your cat may be happy for you to hold their paw and tap the wall with it. After your cat has tapped the wall, speak aloud the price you wish for your home.

Carry your cat or encourage them to follow you into every room of your home and tap a wall in each place. When your cat has tapped the wall with their paw, speak aloud the desired price for your home.

To Prevent Legal Action

This spell is specifically designed to safeguard your assets against legal action.

You will need:
- **7 dried beans**
- **A crossroads**

When your familiar is comfortably settled, seat yourself beside them and put seven dried beans in your mouth. Spit the beans out while speaking the name of the entity or person who is threatening legal action against you. If there is more than one entity or person, use seven more beans for each entity or person.

Pick up the beans and gently drop them onto your cat, saying:

*"Beloved cat, I have spat out the beans,
And will keep what is mine, by honest means."*

Using your fingers, remove the beans from your cat, or pick up your cat so that the beans fall to the floor.

Take the beans to a crossroads and throw them over your left shoulder without looking backward. As you throw them, think or say aloud:

"(Name of entity, entities, person, or people), my cat (their name) and I command you, be gone."

Walk away and do not look back.

That night, take your cat to bed with you and hold them. Speak aloud to tell God or the spirit world what your problem is, and then ask that higher power to deal with your problem for you. From then on, all you need to do is deal with the impending legal situation as time demands.

Purposely do not think of your problem in the meantime because, deprived of the fuel of your thoughts, the problem will dissipate.

To Receive Money You Are Owed

You will need:
- 4 whole star anise pods
- 1 stick of lavender incense in a holder
- 1 white candle
- A little milk in your cat's bowl
- A fountain pen or pen with a nib
- A small piece of white paper
- An unused envelope (optional)

With your familiar at your side, light the lavender incense. Put your cat's bowl, containing a little milk, beside the incense. Place the four star anise pods around the white candle, and then light the candle. Look into the candle flame and say:

*"(Name of corporation or person), you will pay me the money that you owe me.
I give thanks that I have already received it."*

Fill the fountain pen with milk or dip a pen nib into the milk. Write on the piece of white paper the name of the person or corporation owing you the money. Beneath the name, write the owed amount.

Hold the piece of paper near the candle flame, but with enough distance to avoid lighting it on fire, and watch the words and amount that you have written in milk turn brown from the heat. Visualize receiving the money.

When the incense has finished burning, blow out the candle. Fold the piece of paper into three. Throw the remainder of the milk in your cat's bowl away and fill the bowl with fresh water or milk. Keep the piece of paper under your cat's drinking bowl until the money owed to you is repaid. Put the star anise in an envelope to carry in your purse, wallet, or pocket to speed the money's arrival.

Continue to light the white candle every day until it burns to a stub. If you have an open hearth, burn the candle stub. If not, bury the candle stub.

Once the money owed has been paid, bury the star anise and piece of paper that bears the debtor's name and the owed amount.

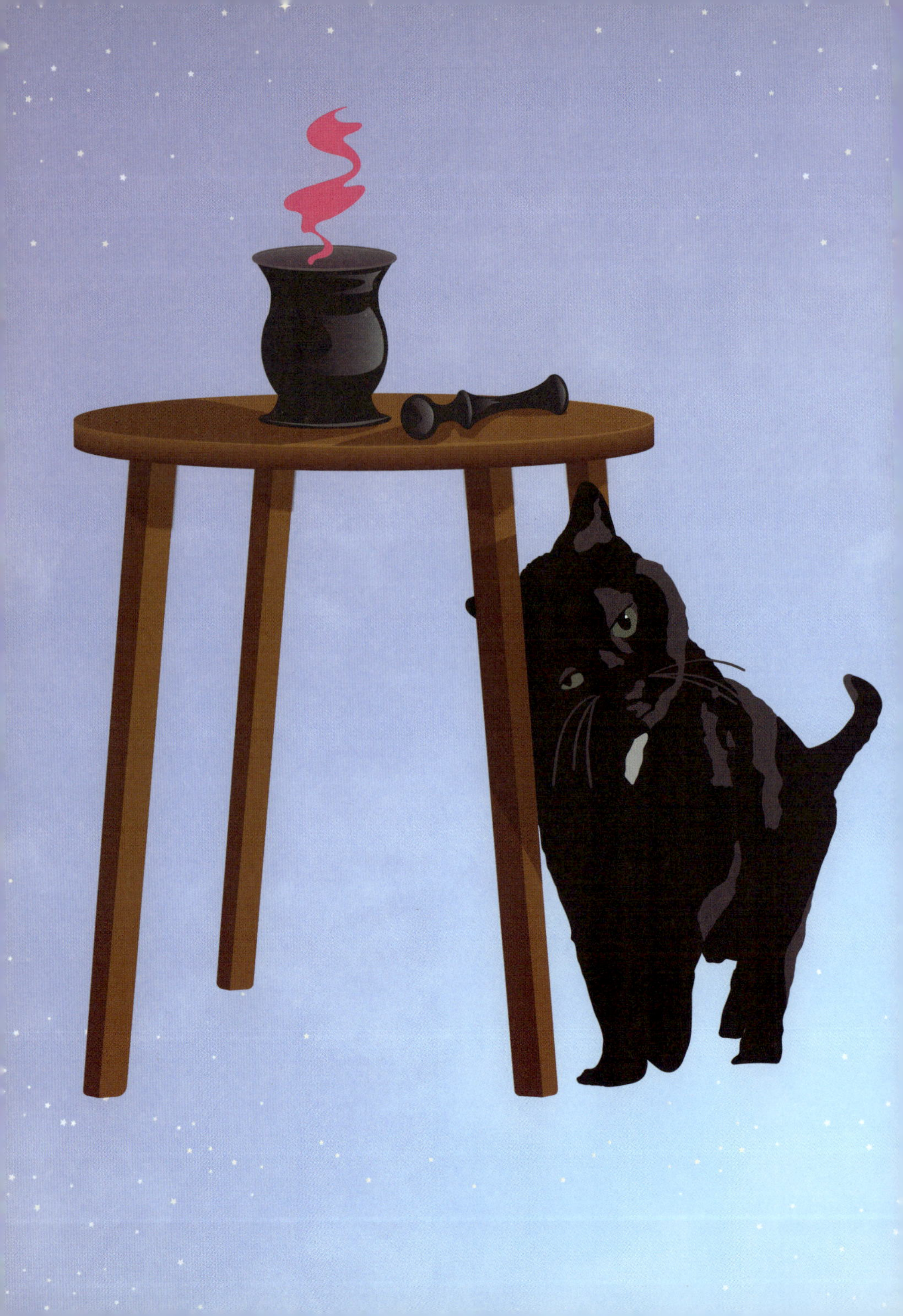

Chapter Six

Spells for Health and Healing

Charms and spells for health have been used for centuries. Being fortunate enough to live in an age of advanced medicine, we rely on them less. But when performed hand in hand with contemporary medicine, healing spells can still do good for people and pets.

The ancient Egyptians believed that cats helped to keep illness away from the home because they kill snakes and vermin. Japanese folk traditions say that a cat placed on an ill person's stomach can cure them. Cat fur has been used in old folk remedies to aid the healing of scalds, burns, and inflammation. People with rheumatism encouraged a cat to sit on their lap or sleep with them so the cat could relieve them of the pain. Some thought that their own pain was transferred to the cat.

In Egyptian tradition, the cat was believed to be the possessor of life because of their connection to the Sun god Horus, who was the source of good health and happiness, and the Eye of Horus (or Ra), which was a symbol representing Horus's powers of well-being and protection. Cat amulets guard our health and safely protect the wearer or property in which the amulet is placed. Egyptian cat talismans also protected the dead.

Most of the spells in this chapter are to be worked by you and your cat in partnership, but a few provide ways for you to protect your cat's health and well-being.

To Heal Your Cat

Bay leaves, ruled by the Sun, represent triumph over adversity.

You will need:
- **Modeling clay**
- **Fur from your cat's brush**
- **A rose quartz crystal (alternatively, a red stone, red rose, or red flower in bloom)**
- **A bay leaf**

Using modeling clay, make a little poppet to resemble your ailing cat. Try to make the model look as much like them as possible. Press some of their brushed-out fur into the modeling clay.

Press the rose quartz into the heart area on the left-hand side of the cat model's chest, thinking as you do so that you wish your cat well. Rose quartz is used because it represents love, is associated with the heart, and because quartz transmits heat, light, and ultraviolet rays. If you cannot get a rose quartz, find a small, shiny red pebble or stone. A fresh rose or other red flower, renewed when it wilts, would also serve your purpose.

Kiss the fresh bay leaf and place your cat model upon it. All cats love the Sun, so place the leaf and model in a comfortable position in your home where the Sun will shine on it.

To Heal Your Cat When You Are Apart

Use this spell when your cat is at the vet, when you are on holiday, or even when you are just away from home for a few hours.

You will need:
- **A magnifying glass**
- **A photograph of your cat**

Hold the magnifying glass an inch or two above the photograph of your cat. You may be quite startled to see that the cat in the photograph appears to come to life. Send strong healing thoughts to your familiar while looking through the magnifying glass and, if you like, also speak to wish them well. Your words have a vibration and resonance that reach much farther than hearing distance.

Sneezing Cat Superstitions

The number of times your cat sneezes are omens.

- If your cat sneezes once, you will be kissed by a stranger. It is also an omen that someone is missing you, as well a sign of a rain shower. (See page 73 for more weather-related omens.)
- Two sneezes, you will receive something good.
- Three sneezes, you will have a cold in three days, but it is also a sign that someone loves you.
- Four sneezes are an omen of marriage.
- Five sneezes predict the birth of a baby boy.
- Six sneezes forecast the birth of a girl.
- Seven sneezes mean you will live a long and fulfilled life.
- If your cat sneezes between midday and midnight, expect good luck.

To Aid Your Cat During a Visit to the Vet

The veterinarian's can be a frightening place. This spell can help your cat be more receptive to the kind of healing offered by the vet.

You will need:
- **A cut glass crystal or prism to reflect rainbow colors**

Stroke your familiar to calm them down. The tactile warmth of your hand stroking their fur, by its soothing effect, helps to heal you and them at the same moment and creates a bond between you.

Move the crystal above your cat's body to shine colored light over their heart. Hold the crystal still for a few moments, then hold the crystal above your cat's head. Focus on sending healing energy into your familiar through the light refracted by the crystal.

Move the crystal from the tip of your cat's nose over their head and down their spine to the tip of your cat's tail and say:

*"You are well, you are healed,
From nose to tail and from tip to tail."*

As you are saying "from tip to tail," move the crystal from your cat's head down to their spine, and from there down all four legs to each paw.

End the spell by holding the crystal over the palm of your other hand so that the colors of the rainbow appear as light upon your own skin.

If either you or your cat is injured or has had an operation, you can aid healing by holding the crystal above the wound for a few minutes so that light shines through the crystal onto the injury or surgical incision.

Afterward, return the crystal to where you keep it or place the crystal inside your pillowcase and sleep with your cat on top of your pillow or bed.

To Heal a Person in Your Presence

A spell like this, worked in front of another person, is best done when your cat has had some experience doing magical work with you.

You will need:
- **A piece of paper**
- **A pen or pencil**
- **A ball of wool**

Place your cat on the lap of the person who is unwell, or put your cat beside the person you wish to heal.

Write the name of the person's illness on a piece of paper. Scrunch the piece of paper up. Roll a ball of wool around the piece of paper. Give the ball of wool to your cat to bat with their paws and chase out the door of the room the unwell person is sitting in.

Afterward, unravel the ball of wool and burn or bury the piece of paper.

Long-Distance Healing

When a far-away someone you care about is ill, you and your familiar can help.

You will need:
- **1 white or blue candle**
- **An upright mirror**

Place a candle in front of an upright mirror, such as a dressing table mirror, making sure that the candle cannot ignite anything. Settle your cat close to you and light the candle. Hold your cat in your arms so that the mirror reflects both of you together. Look into your cat's eyes reflected in the mirror and say:

> *"In the candle flame burning brightly tonight,*
> *(Name of cat) and I send you healing light.*
> *We wish you well, we want you to be.*
> *Get well soon, from kitty and me."*

If at any point your cat wishes to be free from your arms, let them jump down. Continue, with or without your cat, to look in the mirror and visualize the one who is ill made well and happy. Through mental telepathy, send the light reflected in the mirror to the person whom you are healing.

When you are ready, snuff out the candle.

To Heal a Broken Heart

The candle in this spell represents the person whose heart you are trying to heal.

You will need:
- **A sheet of blotting-paper cut into two small pieces**
- **A fountain pen (not ballpoint)**
- **A teaspoonful or two of distilled vinegar in a small dish**
- **Several drops of rose oil**
- **Another small dish**
- **1 blue or white candle**

Write on one of the pieces of paper: *"Heal (name of the person)'s broken heart."* Drop the piece of paper into the dish of vinegar and watch the ink spread and change color. Light the candle and say:

"All bitterness has gone from (name of person)."

Write on another piece of paper: *"(Name of person), whose broken heart is to be healed."* Drop the piece of paper into a clean dish. Sprinkle the piece of paper with a few drops of rose oil and say:

"It is a grace and a gift that (name of person) has forgiven. (Name of person)'s broken heart is healed and they have love in their heart."

Snuff out the candle. Outdoors, bury the piece of paper from the vinegar dish, pouring the vinegar away. Keep the piece of paper on which you sprinkled the rose oil. Give the piece of paper to the person whose broken heart you have healed to drop into their bathwater, or drop it into your own bathwater. Tear the piece of paper into tiny pieces to go down the drain.

If your cat climbs a tree on the day of a death or funeral, they are telling you that the departed soul has gone to Heaven.

To Heal Your Home of Negative Energy

You will need:
- **Your cat's collar with a bell on it, a cat toy with a bell inside, or a handbell**
- **1 red candle**

When your familiar is sitting with their paws on your shoulder, whisper into their left ear what it is that you wish to send out of your home. Then, whisper in your cat's right ear what it is that you wish to welcome in.

Ask your cat to follow you into every room of your home or carry your cat, if they are willing, into every room. In each of the four corners of each room, tinkle the bell on their collar, or remove your cat's collar and shake it in every corner. The ringing bell will dissipate stagnant energies and resonate differently in every room because of the quality of energy at different moments in time. The harmony of the bell will attract good fortune.

Light the red candle in a safe place indoors, close to the door where your cat usually enters your home. When the flame is established, say:

*"With each dainty velvet paw,
Take bad luck away, out through the door.
And wherever you may roam,
Return with good luck for our home."*

Do not leave the candle unattended. When your cat goes out through the door, snuff out the candle.

To Heal a Relationship

This spell must be performed when the Moon is visible—preferably a new moon. It is good to cast outside but can be cast indoors, especially in front of a window where you can see the Moon.

You will need:
- **A hand mirror**

Sit outside at dusk, if possible, with your cat on your lap. Hold the hand mirror so that it reflects the Moon. Look at your cat's eyes and watch their pupils expand from horizontal slits until they look like two full moons.

Spells for Health and Healing

Show your cat their reflection and the Moon's in the mirror and say,

*"Lady Moon of kindness and light,
Heal my relationship with (name of person) tonight.
And may sunshine at the break of day
Bring happiness again, our way."*

Kiss your cat on the head and go indoors with your familiar and the mirror.

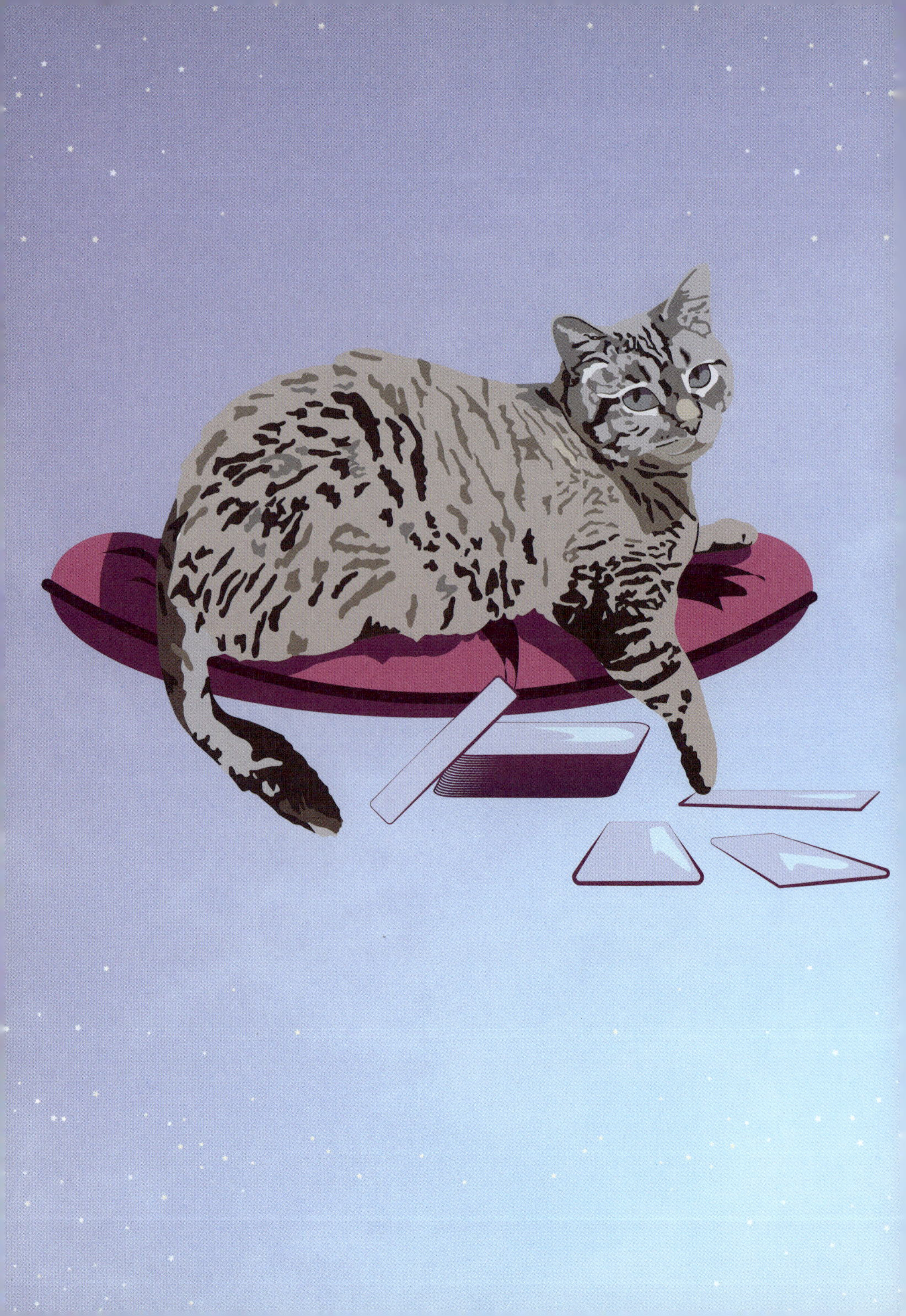

Chapter Seven

Felidomancy: Feline Divination

The Egyptian word for cat is *mau*, meaning "to see." Possessing divine powers and attuned with invisible energy, your cat shows you visible signs through their actions, eyes, body language, moods, and behavior. Your cat is psychic and can help you to become psychic. Their body language is an action reacting to magical knowledge. If you intuitively understand your cat, you can intuitively understand the divine nature of the universe.

You know that your familiar has your best interests at heart and, in their wisdom, knows what is best for you, tells you and expects to be heard, simply because it is well-deserved for both of you. Through your familiar, you can tune in to your own omniscience, meaning "all knowing," and know it all.

By linking to your cat, you too can see as a seer what is evident and what is not. Your cat is a seer, meaning that they can see the clear truth in a given situation. Your cat can, literally and spiritually, see in the dark.

The pupils of your cat's eyes are small in the morning and gradually enlarge during the day until they look like full moons at night. Follow your cat's wisdom: broaden your outlook.

Your familiar will sit with their eyes fixed upon you until you look back and acknowledge their glare. When eye contact is established, you will understand the wordless psychic contact that makes you stop and think, see, and understand what your cat is telling you.

Yes or No Divination

- **Set your cat on your lap and tell your familiar that you wish them to divine your future by answering a question you are about to ask aloud. Ask your familiar to respond by blinking once if the answer to your question is yes, twice for no. Alternatively, ask your familiar to purr an odd number of times for yes and an even number of times for no.**
- **To find the answer to a yes or no question, brush or stroke your cat's tail. Place three hairs from their tail on a piece of paper. Fold up the paper so that the hairs cannot fall out. Put the folded paper under your pillow and sleep on it. In the morning, open the paper. If the three hairs are in the shape of the letter Y, the answer to your question is yes. Any shape other than a Y answers no to your question. Sometimes, the answer comes in a dream while the amulet is under your pillow.**
- **On a small piece of paper, write a question that requires a yes or no answer. Write your cat's name above, below, and on**

Felidomancy: Feline Divination

either side of the question. Scrunch the piece of paper into a ball and place it inside a poppy seed pod. Put the poppy seed pod inside your pillowcase, and the yes or no answer that you seek will be revealed to you in a dream.

- Give a pomegranate to your cat to play with and chase after as if it were a ball. When you are ready to know a yes or no answer to a question, take the pomegranate outdoors. Throw the pomegranate hard on the ground so that it smashes and the seeds fall out. (Be sure to do this on the dirt, not a paved area, and to wear dark-colored clothing since pomegranate juice stains.) Pick up the pomegranate seeds from the ground and count them. An even number of seeds answers yes to your questions, and an odd number of seeds answers no to your question.
- Write your yes or no question on a piece of paper and scrunch the piece of paper into a ball that your cat will bat with their paw. Play with your cat to entice them to chase the ball of paper. If your familiar bats the paper ball more often with their right paw, the answer to your question is yes. The answer is no if they bat the ball of paper more often with their left paw. Alternatively, sit opposite your cat and roll the ball of paper toward them so that they bat it back to you. An even number of times that your cat bats the ball back to you answers yes. An odd number of times answers no to your question.
- Take an oak leaf. Dip it into the water in your cat's bowl. Show the leaf to your cat and ask them to lick the leaf, then place the leaf on a piece of paper. If the leaf dries slowly, the answer is yes. If the leaf dries quickly, the answer is no.
- Your familiar will tell you the answer to your yes or no question if you listen to them drinking their water. With your question

in mind, count how many laps your cat takes. An even number divines the answer yes; an odd number signifies no.
- Take thirteen little scraps of paper torn from a single sheet of paper. Write the word "yes" on six pieces and the word "no" on seven pieces. Scrunch each piece of paper into a small ball. Hold all thirteen wads of paper in your hand and rattle them to encourage your cat to make you open your hand so the papers fall to the floor. Alternatively, place the wads of paper in a pile on the floor and dangle string over them so that your cat leaps onto them, scattering the pile. Pick up the wad that lands farthest away from the others. Smooth the piece of paper in your hand and read yes or no in answer to your question.

They Love Me, They Love Me Not

Place a small handful of cat treats in your cat's dish. After your familiar has eaten, count the number of treats your familiar left. With each treat you count, read one line. The line that coincides with the final treat gives you your answer.

"(first treat) (He/She/They) love(s) me.
(second treat) (He/She/They) love(s) me not.
(third treat) (He/She/They) will want me.
(fourth treat) (He/She/They) won't.
(fifth treat) If (he/she/they) could, (he/she/they) would.
(sixth treat) But (he/she/they) can't."

Will I Get What I Want?

Pour some cat treats into your familiar's dish and leave them there to be eaten. When you later visit your familiar's treat bowl, count the remaining treats, speaking one line for each treat counted:

*"(first treat) I will get what I want.
(second treat) I won't get what I want."*

Repeat until you have counted all of the treats. The last line spoken with the last treat gives you your answer.

Are They a Good Person?

Being highly sensitive, your feline friend can intuitively read a person's character. Your cat's tail will tell you what they think of a person. If the tail and tip are up, your cat is saying that they like the person. Your familiar also approves if their tail curves down with the tip up. If your familiar's tail is slightly raised and slightly curved, your cat is interested without fear. If your cat's tail is up with the tip tilted, they are interested in your friend, but also wary.

It is a sign that a person irritates your familiar if your cat twitches the tip of their tail. When your cat lowers their tail or tucks it behind their hind legs, they are telling you that they feel intimidated by the person. If your familiar arches and bristles their tail, they feel threatened.

Your familiar is telling you that they are fearful if they fluff out their tail fur. If your cat holds their fluffed-up tail high, your cat is telling you that they strongly disapprove of the person you have introduced to them.

Another sign that your familiar disapproves of someone is if they wash themselves vigorously when meeting the person.

Hydromancy

To find which of three potential partners would make you happiest or which of three people will ask you out, ask your cat to reveal the answer with a little hydromancy.

Partially fill three identical bowls with water. Place a basil leaf in one bowl to represent one lover, a rose petal in the second dish to represent the second sweetheart, and an oak leaf in the third bowl to symbolize the third suitor.

The bowl your cat drinks from reveals the one most compatible with you or, as the case may be, the one who will ask you for a date.

Feline Weather Forecasts

Your cat is able to predict how the weather will change within the next few hours. If you read your familiar's signs, you can plan accordingly:

- **If your familiar sharpens their claws on the furniture, good weather is on its way.**
- **"Cat on its brain is a sign of rain." Expect rain if your familiar curls up with the back of their head flat on the furniture or floor, with their chin in the air.**
- **If your cat licks their feet, head, and whiskers, then over and behind their ears, rain will soon fall.**
- **When your cat sneezes once, expect a rain shower. (See page 58 for more omens from cat sneezes.)**
- **It is also said to be a forecast of rain if your cat sits staring out of the window.**

Sailors draw omens from a cat's behavior. "Cat's paw" is a nautical expression meaning a light breeze.

- **A cat mewing on board is a sign of a gale.**
- **A cat scratching on wood, such as a door frame or table leg, or even its own scratching post, is a sign of rough weather because the cat is thought to be "raising a storm."**
- **High winds and storms are forecast if your cat frolics and jumps as if suddenly bitten by a flea.**

- "The cat has a gale of wind in their tail." Anticipate gales and storms if your cat is frisky and twitches their tail quickly.
- If your cat sits with their tail to the fire, it is an omen of frost and a spell of cold weather.

Are You Familiar with Your Familiar?

The eyes have it: cat's pupils shine in the dark and reflect light at dawn and dusk, as well as in other moments of low light. "Cat's-Eye," the semiprecious opalescent mineral gem, has acquired its name because it possesses chatoyancy, changing shine and color like cat's eyes in the dark.

Cats are nocturnal hunters, and their eyes glow in the dark because they absorb more light than human eyes. Unlike humans, cats have a mirror-like layer behind the retina that reflects light to the retinal cells.

Your feline is "the cat's whiskers" or "the cat that got the cream" when telling you a few mundane and magical things you might not already know about them.

- **By a whisker:** Your familiar has twelve whiskers in four horizontal rows on each side of their nose. The twenty-four whiskers are more than sensitive detectors that tell a cat whether a gap is wide enough for their body to enter and exit without getting stuck; whiskers are surrounded by nerve endings that detect air currents and solid objects without contact, enabling your familiar to hunt as skillfully by night

as by day. When cats hunt, they wind their whiskers around their prey to detect whether the victim is dead or alive.
- Your familiar moves their whiskers forward when inquisitive and backward when wary. The top two rows can move in unison and out of sync with the bottom two rows, and the middle rows are the most sensitive of all.
- Purring: Cats begin purring as week-old kittens to let their mother cat know they are receiving the milk she is feeding them. She responds by purring back. Cats in a friendly, contented mood purr to say they feel sociable, as well as to say thank you. But cats in pain also purr to ask for help.
- The cat's meow: A cat's meow is said to consist of sixty-three notes. This may be the origin of lore about communication between a witch and their familiar. The witch's cat was said to speak the language of its mistress; one witch, Moll White, owned a tabby who was reputed to have spoken in English on several occasions.
- Cat tails: Cats use their tails to communicate with you. Your familiar waves their tail from side to side when they are feeling indecisive.
- Cat tail cures: The tip of your cat's tail brushed on a wart is said to make it wither and disappear. It is believed that a sty on the eyelid will disappear quickly if you brush it with the tip of a black cat's tail while reciting this age-old saying:

"I poke thee,
I don't poke thee.
I poke the queff that's under thee,
O qualway, qualway."

Your Cat's Aura

Your cat has an aura, or glowing emanation. It is most easily visible if the background is plain rather than colored wallpaper. About an inch from their body, you will see white or golden light. Beyond that, still flowing in the shape of your cat, is a misty color extending outward about twelve inches.

A change of mood can alter your cat's aura from one color to another, until their state of mind returns to its usual disposition. A zigzag flash, similar to a lightning flash, can appear in your familiar's aura if something suddenly excites, shocks, or frightens them.

The colors and key words listed below tell you your cat's nature and what they predict about your immediate future based on their aura.

- **Red:** Your familiar is strong-willed, possessing a great love for life. They are passionate and very affectionate. A feral familiar with a red aura may suddenly become aggressive because red is the color of blood and fire. Key words: *lusty, strong, courageous, powerful.*
- **Gold:** The overruling nature of the cat whose aura is gold is one of goodness, intelligence, and consideration. In your familiar, you possess a treasure beyond earthly wealth because gold is the color of the highest spirituality, as well as majesty. Key words: *divine, spiritual, healthy.*
- **Orange:** You have a precious and very special cat. They are uncommonly wise, affectionate, and cheerful, possessing a loving heart and a great sense of humor. Because orange is the color of the Sun, which brings illumination and life,

your familiar will bring light and happiness into your life and home. Key words: *successful, happy, fun, cleansing.*
- Yellow: Your familiar is highly intelligent and spiritual. Because yellow is the color of the Sun when it is warm but not dangerously hot, your familiar lifts your mood to a happier, brighter, more peaceful state of mind. Key words: *psychic, divinatory, wise, visionary, enlightening.*
- Green: Your cat has a kind, sweet, freedom-loving nature. They are emotionally independent because green is the color of nature. More often than not, your cat will like to sit where they can see outdoors. Cats with green auras are procreators who make excellent parents and show cats because they like exhibiting their talents. Key words: *lucky, prosperous, beautiful, youthful, faithful.*
- Blue: Your familiar is a natural healer who is warm, calm, loyal, and affectionate. They exchange their knowledge with you because they have a deep desire for you to understand them more intimately. Key words: *healing, peaceful, relaxing, calming, teaching, guiding.*
- Indigo: Your familiar loves peace and harmony and may often appear to focus on things in the room that are invisible to you. They are sensitive to your moods and act in accordance to them. Key words: *powerful, spiritual, omnipotent, loving.*
- Violet: Your familiar is psychic, forever youthful, and eager to entertain new people in your home or welcome a change of residence and routine. They will teach you things about yourself in a most uncanny way. Key words: *sensitive, pure, spiritually protective, sagely, affectionate.*
- Black: A black aura is a sign that your familiar has experienced sadness or danger and is in need of love, reassurance,

and safety. Key words: *good luck, opposites, attraction, stability, endurance, strength.*
- **Silver:** Your very spiritual familiar is extremely perceptive, possessing a strong love link to you and to the invisible world. By tuning in to your familiar, you will find that you are in sync with destiny: the right people and situations will appear, bringing good fortune, unexpected luck, and precisely what you require at a particular time. **Key words:** *intuitive, honest, sensitive, strong, feminine, warm, loving, giving.*

Magical Cat Wishing Pouches

You and your cat, divided by time and geographical distance, can remain linked if you carry a magical cat wishing pouch. Through it, you are bound as one because something that has been in contact with a person or animal retains that connection.

A magical cat wishing pouch is a little bag filled with herbs, spices, and various objects of symbolic or magical significance. Carry the wishing pouch in your purse or pocket, or sleep with it under your pillow. You must light a white candle to represent purity when filling your wishing pouch for the first time.

You could put the ingredients in a little cloth purse you already possess. Alternatively, you can make a wishing pouch by placing the ingredients in the center of a handkerchief, gathering the cloth around them, and tying them up into a bundle with a ribbon or cord. Another method is to cut a circle of felt. Glue a much smaller circle of cardboard

Felidomancy: Feline Divination

in the center of the felt circle. Punch an even number of holes around the outer edge of the felt, and thread the ribbon or cord through them to make a drawstring pouch.

The ingredients for your pouch should include a hair from your head and fur from your cat's brush. You can also add teeth or claws your familiar has naturally shed. By carrying your cat's personal teeth or claws, you are not severed from your cat, even though you may be apart.

You could also add a little cat-shaped pebble or stone that you find, because you are attracted to it, when you are out for a walk.

You should put a lucky charm into the bag: a photograph of your cat or a small drawing that represents something that you know or feel about your cat or your cat's behavior or astrological sign.

In addition to maintaining your connection with your cat when you are apart, the wishing pouch can be used for magic. For luck in love, you should insert a few dried rose petals or rose buds. To attract healthy communication, add some lavender or, if you prefer, a whole nutmeg. Whenever you wish for something to happen, write your wish in ink on a bay leaf and put the bay leaf into the wishing pouch. To attract love, add seven apple seeds and some thyme, if you have it. For sexual potency, add a few dried beans or an oak leaf. To increase your psychic powers, include a few star anise pods and peppermint or spearmint leaves. For protection and purification, add a sprig of rosemary or some dried rosemary or a bay leaf.

A kitten born on Michaelmas Eve, September 28, or on Michaelmas Day, September 29, at the end of blackberry season, was in Britain affectionately known as a "Michaelmas kitten" or a "blackberry cat." The owner of a Michaelmas kitten should expect it to be unusually playful and mischievous.

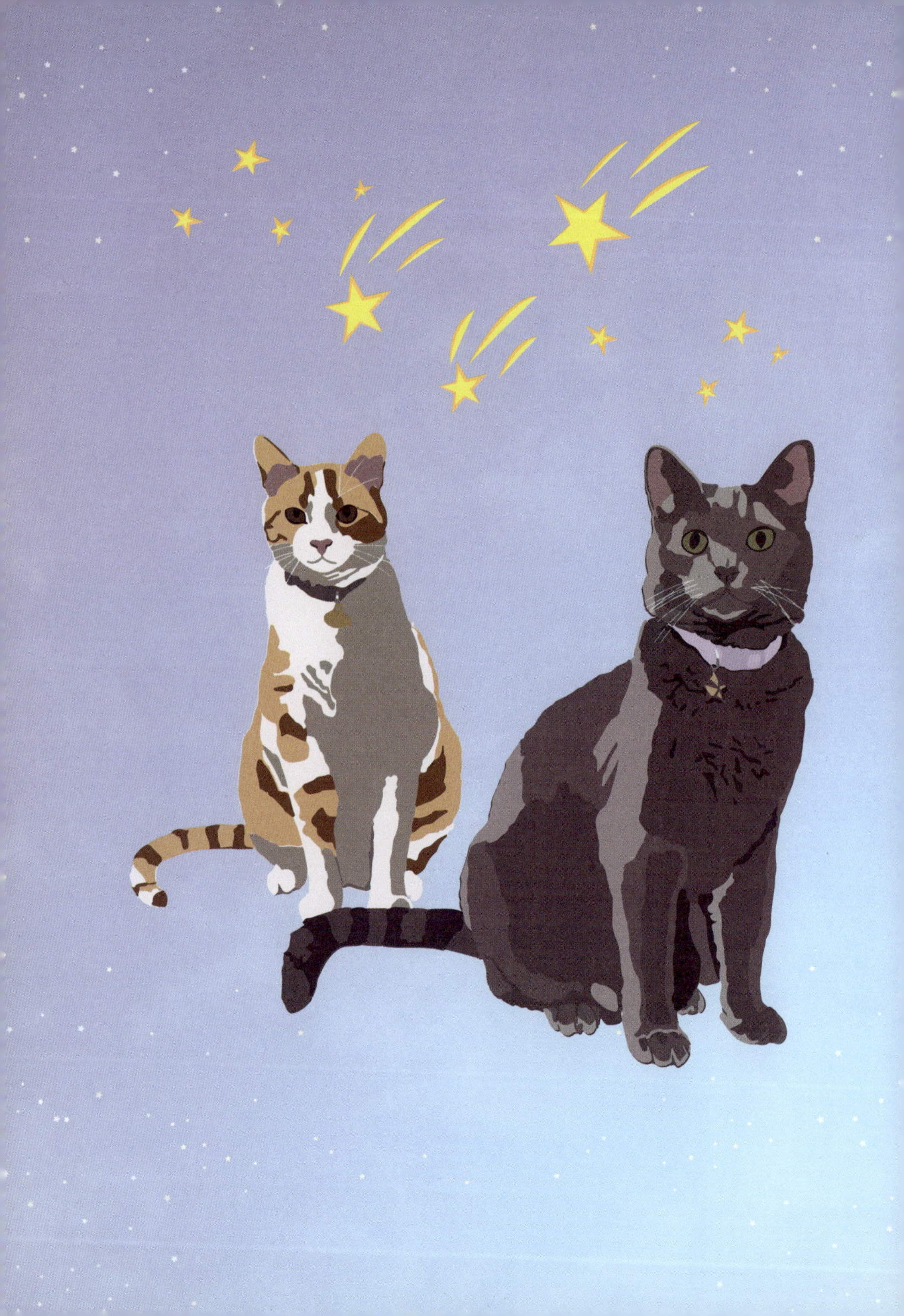

Chapter Eight

Know Your Cat by Their Astrological Sign

You can cast a spell according to your cat's astrological birth sign to join the two of you together as working magical partners, bonding your cat as your familiar. First thing in the morning and last thing at night, say good morning and good night to your cat. Your friendship and theirs should be appreciated and not taken for granted by either of you.

The characteristics of each sign are described here, and for each sign there is a spell you can use to initiate your cat as your familiar. Also listed are stones you can both wear to link yourselves psychically; you can also choose a collar of the stone's color for your cat.

If you know the date of your cat's birth, you will know their birth sign, which would be the same astrological sign as for a person born on that date. If you buy or acquire a kitten, you can discover the birth sign by counting the number of weeks of their age backward to the date of birth. Kittens usually are taken from their mother cat at about six to eight weeks of age.

If you have no idea of your cat's date of birth, reading the following descriptions will help you determine whether your cat is ruled by an Air, Fire, Water, or Earth sign, which in turn will help you deduce your cat's most probable birth sign.

Your Cat is Ruled by Air
(Gemini, Libra, and Aquarius)

Your familiar is lean, tense, perceptive, clever, nervous, humorous, attention-seeking, and restless. They enjoy watching your activities, television, and the environment outside the window or door. Your familiar's mood is fickle and as changeable and difficult to grasp as the wind. They are playing paws up in the air at one moment and curled up asleep the next, jumping from "entertaining star of the show" to enjoying their own company.

⭐ Gemini Cat ⭐

- **May 21–June 21**
- **Key phrase: I instinctively know my intuition is correct.**
- **Stone or collar colors: Agate; turquoise.**

Gemini cats are the perfect familiar because they need a soul mate. They are fast learners, easily housetrained, good fun, playful, talkative, always active, and full of nervous energy. Being ruled by the planet Mercury, they dart around with mercurial speed and are full of surprises.

You get two for the price of one with dual-natured Gemini cats. They are inquisitive, versatile, loving, and highly intelligent. Their sharp minds make them entertaining because they love being the center of attention. They are fussy—not greedy—about food and need variety in their diet. Because they enjoy life outdoors, when indoors, they need plenty to amuse their mentally active brains. Love is the answer.

Gemini cats could go astray more often than other cats. They may follow you down the road and would like wearing a cat harness to accompany you on walks.

Bonding Spell for a Gemini Familiar

Caraway, mint, and lavender are all ruled by the planet Mercury, which governs your Gemini familiar. Wednesday is ruled by the planet Mercury, so Wednesday would be the best day on which to cast your spell.

You will need:
- **1 yellow or gold candle**
- **A pen or straight pin**
- **A flowerpot filled with potting soil**
- **A few lavender flower heads**
- **A handkerchief or scrap of cloth**
- **A few pinches of caraway seeds**
- **Some fur taken from your cat's brush**
- **A yellow ribbon or thread**
- **A mint plant**

Writing lengthwise on the candle, inscribe with a pen or straight pin your cat's name, followed by your full name. Put the candle in the flowerpot on the table. Settle your cat beside you and light the candle.

Strip the lavender heads, letting the buds fall into the center of the handkerchief or scrap of cloth. Add the caraway seeds and cat fur. Lift the edges of the cloth up to tie the ingredients into a bundle using the yellow ribbon or thread.

Sit with the candle while it burns through both your inscribed names. Snuff the candle out. Sleep that night with the bundle under your pillow and your cat on top of your bed. Afterward, keep the handkerchief among your personal possessions or close to you.

The following day, bury the candle stub in your garden and plant the mint on top of it. Alternatively, push the candle stub into the flowerpot and plant the mint on top of it. As the mint thrives, so too will your bond with your familiar. The mint will keep your relationship fresh and lively.

⭐ Libra Cat ⭐

- **September 23–October 23**
- **Key phrase: I exude peace and harmony.**
- **Stone or collar color: Opal.**

Your Libra familiar is a brilliant companion for your spells because they are happiest being the fireside cat. Libra cats like a peaceful home. Because harmony and justice are essential to their nature, they are very loving, instinctively knowing what is fair to you and to them. They understand what you say to them and learn easily.

Libra cats have a clean, well-balanced, beautiful body and refined features. They like company and will be friendly to you, your friends, and other pets you may have. Their good looks, sociability, and need for pampering make them successful candidates for cat shows. They love being groomed.

Libra familiars are indecisive with food and find it hard to make up their minds about what tastes best. Although they may appear serene, they are inwardly nervous and need to be treated with sensitivity and kindness. They may react to household arguments by not eating a meal because the stress of it has made them lose their appetite.

Should your familiar turn their attention to another member of the family, do not look upon it as disloyalty. It is because they have so much love to give and want everybody to be happy.

Bonding Spell for a Libra Familiar

Friday is governed by Venus, your familiar's ruling planet, so Friday would be the best day on which to cast a spell to unite you and your familiar as a magical working team. All the ingredients are also governed by the planet.

You will need:
- **1 pale blue or pale pink candle**
- **2 small pieces of paper**
- **2 red roses**
- **A pen with blue ink**
- **A vase filled with water**
- **An apple**
- **A straight pin**
- **A pear**
- **Pale pink or pale blue ribbon or thread**

Settle your cat so that they are with you when you cast your spell. Light the candle and place it on a table. On one of the two small pieces of paper, write your cat's name in cursive writing with the blue pen, followed by your own name. Fold the piece of paper in half to enclose the names. Put the folded paper on the table to the right of the candle. Place the two red roses in the vase and put the vase on top of the folded paper.

Take the apple and, using the dressmaking pin, prick your cat's name followed by your own name into the skin. Place the apple to the right of the candle.

On the remaining small piece of paper, write your cat's name in cursive writing and join your own name to theirs. Cut the pear in half and place the piece of paper bearing both names between the two halves of the pear. Bind the two pear halves together with the pale pink or blue ribbon or thread, and place the pear in front of the candle.

Show the apple to your cat and let them see you eat it, including the core if you can. Snuff out the candle.

The following day, bury the pear in your garden or in some open space.

⭐ Aquarius Cat ⭐

- **January 20–February 18**
- **Key phrase: I create the magic we invent.**
- **Stone or collar colors: Amethyst, aquamarine.**

Unique Aquarius familiars are sweet-natured, very spiritual, highly intelligent, and inventive in the way they bond with you. Aquarius cats are likely to tell you where their special bed or food should be placed in your home. The chances are it will be where they can see you and what you are up to.

Though genuinely loyal to you, your Aquarius familiar will at times appear to be emotionally distant. Make sure that your familiar knows where they live so they can find their way home. Loving everyone and everything, they will like exploring outdoors. Aquarius cats may stroll into other homes around the neighborhood and make themselves quite at home there. They may also invite neighborhood cats into your home.

Being bright, they may discover a way to unlock the cat flap or open a cupboard door. When you show attention to other people or pets, your familiar may jealously rebel and show distaste by shredding your furniture.

Aquarius cats are unlikely to pine should you go away on vacation. Instead, they will form a relationship with their caregiver and other pets who are around. In your absence, they will amuse themselves and, upon your return, be exceptionally loving and not at all resentful.

Bonding Spell for an Aquarius Familiar

Holly leaves, comfrey, and electric blue are all ruled by Uranus, which rules Aquarius. The folk name for the pansy is "heartsease," representing love and affection between two beings.

You will need:
- **1 electric blue or silver candle**
- **Comfrey tea**
- **Some pansies growing in a pot**
- **A holly leaf or piece of paper cut into the shape of a holly leaf**
- **A pen with blue ink to cast your spell**

Make yourself a cup of comfrey tea and take it to where you are going to cast your spell. Settle your cat close to you. Place the potted pansies beside the electric blue or silver candle, and light the candle. When the flame is established, speak your cat's name, followed by your own name, three times. Sip the comfrey tea until it is finished.

Write on the holly leaf your cat's name in cursive writing, followed by yours. Press the holly leaf into the soil in which the pansies are growing.

Look into the candle flame and say:

> *"As the candle burns,*
> *(Cat's name and yours)*
> *Become one in*
> *The light of love."*

When you feel ready, snuff out the candle.

The following day, plant the pansies on top of the holly leaf in a window box or your garden. Alternatively, keep the potted pansy indoors. In the fullness of time, as the pansies grow, your relationship with your familiar will flower.

Your Cat is Ruled by Earth (Taurus, Virgo, and Capricorn)

Your familiar is reticent, stubborn, and a creature of habit. They are upset when you change their routine or neglect to give them attention. Being territorial and predictable, they will never forsake you when you need reassurance. Practical and materialistic, they like you to be home with them.

⭐ Taurus Cat ⭐

- **April 20–May 20**
- **Key phrase: I possess you, as your familiar.**
- **Stone or collar color: Emerald.**

Your Taurean familiar is loyal, comforting, and able to guide you out of yourself.

Taurean cats have thick necks, a solid stature, and a particularly furry tuft between their ears. Their eyes are intense and staring. Their nature is patient, affectionate, practical, and persistent. As a creature of habit, they are upset by changes in routine. Taurean familiars may be slow to learn but will retain what they are taught.

Being fond of food, Taurean cats may bully or cajole you into overfeeding them. Taurean cats like to be the boss and will dominate other pets in the household.

Preferring the luxury of home, they will not take kindly to being put in a cattery; they think they are too special, which is true. Stubborn Taurean cats do not like to be forced to do anything. They enjoy freedom of decision and when it is denied them, they may fly into a temper. They have robust health and generally prefer life in the countryside. They are devoted, reliable, and deserving of appreciation and love, which includes sleeping on your bed and the best food you can afford.

Bonding Spell for a Taurus Familiar

The pink rose, ribbon, candle, and peach—all governed by the planet Venus, which rules Taurus—will empower your bond with your familiar.

You will need:
- 1 pink candle (if your familiar is female) or blue candle (if your familiar is male)
- A peach
- A pink rose
- A pink ribbon or thread

Settle your familiar beside you and light the candle. Cut the peach in half and remove the pit. Place the stem of the rose between the peach halves while saying:

"Nothing divides my familiar (name of cat) and me. Only love is between us."

Bind the two peach halves together with the pink ribbon or thread. Stroke your cat and sit with the candle until you feel ready to snuff the candle out.

When you have extinguished the candle, bury the peach and rose in your garden or an open space.

⭐ Virgo Cat ⭐

- **August 22–September 22**
- **Key phrase: I am your truly devoted familiar.**
- **Stone or collar colors: Chrysolite, peridot.**

Beloved Virgo cats will show they love to be with you by constantly shadowing your side. They are extremely reliable critics because they know you better than you think. They are often very vocal, neat and tidy, and extremely clean. They are easily housetrained.

Pay attention to what they are trying to tell you, because Virgo familiars are great communicators. A Virgo cat I know soiled on her owner's husband's trousers to say she didn't think much of the husband who was having an affair that she knew about before the wife did.

Virgo cats are choosy about food and unlikely to have a big appetite. They are meticulously fussy, thriving on nervous energy and in need of constant fuss and pampering. They may try to get you off your phone or sit on your work so that you pay more attention to them. Though very sociable, they have an independent streak and, spur of the moment, may suddenly fly out of the room to have their own personal space or to be with another person or pet in your home.

Virgo familiars have a great sense of humor and, for fun, may suddenly pounce on you from a hiding place. Or when you are trying to sew on a button, they may run off with the cotton reel.

Bonding Spell for a Virgo Familiar

Yellow and white are ruled by the planet Mercury, which governs Virgo.

You will need:
- **1 yellow candle**
- **3 white candles**
- **1–2 paper clips**
- **A photograph of your cat**
- **A photograph of yourself**

Settle your familiar close to you where they can see you cast your spell. Place the two photographs face up and side by side on your table. Put the four candles, one yellow and three white, around the photos.

Light the four candles, beginning with the yellow one. As you light each candle, speak your cat's name followed by your own name and the words:

"We are at one with each other."

Take the two photographs and place them face to face so that your cat is looking at you and you are looking at your cat. Clip the photographs together with the paper clips.

Sit with the candles while they burn for a little while, and then snuff them out. Sleep with the photographs inside your pillowcase or keep them forever in a bedside drawer.

Capricorn Cat

- **December 22–January 19**
- **Key phrase: I am your familiar, you are mine.**
- **Stone or collar colors: Garnet, ruby.**

Capricorn familiars are very faithful. Although they are well-mannered and sociable, they are unlikely to show as much affection to others as they do to you. They are serious, even as kittens, about wanting to play with you rather than be amused by toys. You will notice that they like to climb to a high position, whether it is up trees or on top of furniture. They do not take risks or play with life. They are rather pensive cats but have a very good sense of humor.

Loyal Capricorn cats like routine and meals fed punctually at the same time each day. They are not fussy eaters and will let little go to waste. These homebodies love to stay close by rather than wander far when let out. They retain a youthful appearance their whole life long and often have a look of sadness even though they are happy.

Capricorn cats are extraordinarily kind and considerate to children and the elderly. Relationships with your Capricorn familiars will be close because they will behave as if they understand every word spoken to them. They particularly need affection and praise to help them overcome an inborn shyness, sometimes seen as timidity. They are musical, so do not be surprised if their meow sounds rather like a song.

Bonding Spell for a Capricorn Familiar

In the language of flowers, ivy means "I will always cling to you." As the ivy grows, your bond with your familiar will strengthen. Both the color brown and ivy are ruled by the planet Saturn, which governs your familiar's birth sign.

You will need:
- **1 dark brown candle**
- **An ivy plant in a pot**
- **Some fur from your cat's brush**

Call your familiar to your side. Place the ivy plant to the right of the brown candle. Light the candle.

Brush your familiar's fur so that they purr. To the rhythm of your cat's purr, say:

"We are bound as one and cling together in magical love."

Take your familiar's fur from the brush and press it into the soil in which the ivy is growing. When you feel the time is right, snuff the candle. Keep the ivy plant indoors or planted out in your garden.

Your Cat is Ruled by Fire (Aries, Leo, and Sagittarius)

For no apparent reason, Fire cats frenziedly fly around the room or out the door. They appear to have a playful sense of humor and try to bring out the fun in you. Your familiar has a fiery enthusiasm for bright flames and sunshine, and a burning desire to impress people. They are dominant and willful regarding other cats or pets, as well as an independent, fearless, and avid hunter.

⭐ Aries Cat ⭐

- **March 21–April 19**
- **Key phrase: I want my own way immediately as your familiar.**
- **Stone or collar colors: Diamond, ruby.**

Aries familiars are flirtatious with other cats (and people, too). Being overly active, they demand a lot of your time and attention. They have a very big meow and often red or ginger-colored fur. They insist on their own way and are impatient with you to give them what they want. When you disappoint them, they show their emotion by clawing furniture, your clothes, or even you. Because Aries cats are fearless, they are accident-prone as kittens and, when older, tend to rush into scraps with other cats.

Ruled by fire, they are attracted to flames, such as log fires, candles, and gas burners. They are adventurous "cat-burglars," and may raid your neighbor's kitchen, trash, or bird feeder for food, seizing trophies that—embarrassingly for you—they may drag through your cat flap or leave in your garden for the neighbors to see.

Being strong-willed, Aries familiars may not always come to you when called. But they are cuddly as kittens and such lovable rogues when adults that you are likely to love them for their outstanding antics.

Bonding Spell for an Aries Familiar

The planet Mars will align you and your cat's energy because it rules allspice and the red candle and stone.

You will need:
- **1 red candle**
- **A plate**
- **A red stone**
- **Ground allspice**

With your familiar close to you, place the candle in a holder on a plate. When your familiar is settled, put the red stone beside your cat so that the stone is touching their fur. Light the candle, stroke your cat, and look into the flame.

When your cat is purring or settled, sprinkle a few pinches of allspice into the candle flame and say:

> *"(Name of cat), I love you and you love me,*
> *Bound in magic we will always be.*
> *I am yours and you are mine,*
> *My perfect, Aries familiar feline."*

When you are ready, snuff out the candle. Keep the red stone in a spell box or bedside drawer.

⭐ Leo Cat ⭐

- **July 23–August 22**
- **Key phrase: I need to create.**
- **Stone or collar colors: Gold, amber; topaz.**

Leo familiars love basking in the Sun and are unlikely to demand to go outside when it is raining for fear of getting their magnificent fur coat wet. Leo cats often have almost mane-like neck fur and large amber eyes.

Leo cats are proud and haughty and often large and lazy. They look positively indignant when asked to move from the most comfortable seat in the house or from their spot stretched out on the floor, exactly where you need to walk. The Leo familiar rules your home and your life like a monarch. Leos like life's luxuries, such as large portions of the most expensive food. They would not think of sleeping alone, only on your bed, because they seek warmth and comfort. Ruled by the Sun, your Leo cat may overdo lying in sunshine all day, perhaps resulting in sunburned ears and nose. They like attention and will seek it from you, your guests, and your neighbors too. If you have other pets, your Leo familiar will make sure they are at the top of the pecking order.

Leo cats are particularly caring parents who are very protective and attentive to their kittens, who often arrive in big litters.

Bonding Spell for a Leo Familiar

For this Sun sign, use an orange or yellow candle and a bay leaf, both ruled by the Sun. You can clean lipstick from your cat's paws with a cotton ball or tissue and warm water.

You will need:
- **1 orange or yellow candle**
- **2 pieces of white paper**
- **Lemon juice squeezed from a fresh lemon**
- **Lipstick (orange-colored would be the most appropriate)**
- **A bay leaf**
- **A new envelope or handkerchief**

Light the candle. Fill the fountain pen with lemon juice or dip the pen nib into the lemon juice to write on the first piece of paper: *"My cat (name) and I are one forever."* Write the date below.

Write your cat's name, your name, and your address in lemon juice on the second piece of white paper.

Put lipstick on your familiar's left front paw and press their paw to the front, shiny side of the bay leaf, to take your cat's left paw print. Put lipstick on your familiar's right front paw and press it to the back of the bay leaf.

Hold the first piece of paper close enough to the candle flame to the heat, but not close enough to burn the paper. The words that you have written in lemon juice will turn brown.

Put the second piece of paper, along with the bay leaf, in a clean envelope or handkerchief. Keep it safely in your purse or wallet where you will see it often or, alternatively, among your most intimate possessions.

Snuff out the candle. When your familiar is ready, cuddle them or take them to bed for the night.

⭐ Sagittarius Cat ⭐

- **November 22–December 21**
- **Key phrase: I am daring, adventurous, and humorous.**
- **Stone or collar color: Turquoise.**

Your Sagittarius familiar is fun, loving life and you. If ever there was a cat born with nine lives, it is the Sagittarius, born under the luck-bringing sign of Jupiter. Because the Archer is the hunter, your familiar loves chasing prey in the great outdoors, whether it is a bird, human, or another cat. They prefer the chase to the kill and have a tendency to stray or wander. They are generally sleek and lean, and may incur the occasional scrape during their adventures. Active indoors, your familiar will entertain you with athletics, and although your cat may always land on their feet, objects may not land unharmed.

Your familiar is a little person. Their happy-go-lucky enthusiasm toward you will show you that they think you make a good team. Their intuition is strong and will tune into anything you want them to. Always in a good mood, your Sagittarius cat cannot understand why other people are not as high spirited, and they'll do what they can to try to make everyone happy. They are not territorial and will be quite happy to share hearth and home with other pets. Your freedom-loving Sagittarius familiar is a great but independent companion who will warm your home and life with their bright, amusing presence.

Bonding Spell for a Sagittarius Familiar

You will need:
- **2 acorns or 2 oak leaves**
- **1 blue candle**
- **1 crimson candle**
- **A small tin to keep the acorns in**

Light both candles. Hold one acorn in your cat's left paw and the other in their right. One acorn represents you, and the other acorn represents your familiar. An acorn is symbolic of strength.

Look at the light of the candle flame and, while holding your familiar's paws, say:

> *"In spells, we link through love as one,*
> *May our bond be happy and good fun.*
> *I am your familiar and you are mine,*
> *Our duty to each other until the end of time."*

Snuff out the candles and keep the two acorns in a tin, because the acorns are ruled by Jupiter, which rules your Sagittarius cat. As time goes by, you can add shed claws, whiskers, or milk teeth to the tin. Holding the tin and contents will establish a psychic link between you and your cat. Try telepathically calling your cat to you by holding the tin.

Your Cat is Ruled by Water (Pisces, Cancer, and Scorpio)

These familiars are sensitive and emotionally dependent upon you and seems to intuitively know your behavior and actions in advance. They are secretive and psychic, seeing things that are invisible to you. Water cats' personalities run deep. They like to sit by water, whether it is a garden pond, a cup of tea, a shower, or a bath. They are defensive but rarely attack.

Pisces Cat

- **February 19–March 20**
- **Key phrase: I, your familiar, am a dreamer.**
- **Stone or collar color: Pearl.**

Pisces familiars are very gentle, sensitive, and loving, and are likely to be more psychic than other felines. They are delicate in nature and easily upset. They may turn their back on you when laughed at or chastised.

They are slow to housetrain and likely to be untidy, particularly as kittens and in old age. Pisces cats often have a round face and round eyes with a faraway gaze. They dislike solitude and enjoy the company of humans and other household pets. They are kind but liable to take a swipe when angered.

Water is a magnet to Pisces cats, who will more than likely watch you when you are washing your hair or taking a bath or shower. They may acquire the skill to drink water from the kitchen tap or bathroom, so be careful to avoid potential accidents.

If there are upheavals at home, such as painting or decorating, they will find somewhere quiet to sleep for a while. If you move, be extra careful that your Pisces familiar does not get lost, because they like to wander.

Bonding Spell for a Pisces Familiar

You will need:
- **1 silver candle**
- **A dish of clean, fresh water**
- **A gray pebble or a shell**

Settle your cat in the room in which you are going to cast your spell. Light the silver candle and place the dish of water in front of it.

Rub your cat's tail along your hand, down between the first and second fingers, then up again between the second and third fingers, and down between the third and fourth finger. While you do that, say:

> *"I love your purr,*
> *I love your soft fur.*
> *In life we are one,*
> *The magic has begun."*

Put the gray pebble or shell to your cat's nose for them to sniff and see. Encourage your cat to breathe life into the pebble or shell with their breath. Then drop the pebble or shell into the dish of water.

Stroke and talk to your cat while you sit and watch the candle burn. When you feel the moment is right, snuff out the candle. Remove the pebble or shell and dry it to keep close to you or among your personal possessions. Use the water for your bath or shower, or for washing your hair.

⭐ Cancer Cat ⭐

- **June 22–July 22**
- **Key phrase: I am your familiar, we nurture each other.**
- **Stone or collar colors: Moonstone, pearl.**

Cancerian familiars, with eyes like the full moon at night, are potent helpers in spellcasting because they are ruled by the Moon, which is visible at night when many spells are cast. They are the most cat-like of all cats because the Moon rules the cat kingdom as a whole. Your familiar's eyes are also more Moon-like than any other cat's eyes. You will probably notice Cancerian cats staring into thin air, mysteriously following something with their eyes that is invisible to you, or playing with something you cannot see. These are very psychic cats. Cancerian familiars possess a sixth sense about you, your family, your home, and those dearest to you.

They love home and creature comforts. Being territorial, they are easily domesticated and quickly adapt to home and lifestyle changes, including a move. They are likely to communicate with you telepathically and understand your changing moods. Their meow is often faint and delicate, like their features.

Cancerian cats are sensitive and emotional and will be utterly devoted to you. They have crabby moods and withdraw into solitude for reasons you can never know. Telepathically, Cancerian familiars sense when you are taking them to the vet or going on vacation, even before they have seen the cat carrier or your suitcase.

Having a strong, emotional, loving attachment to you, Cancerian familiars will probably go off their food while you are away. When you return, they will not close their eyes, point their nose in the air, turn their head, and walk away from you, as if to say, "you deserted me." Instead, a warm welcome with a lot of purring awaits you.

Bonding Spell for a Cancerian Familiar

Perform this spell when the Moon is full.

You will need:
- **1 white or silver candle**
- **A white lily, or another white flower or blossom**

Light the candle. Hold your cat to your heart so that you feel or hear both your hearts beating as one. Making sure that the candle is burning safely, carry your cat to a window or into your garden where you can see the full moon.

Wait for your cat to put their front paws over your left shoulder or place them there. Kiss their ears, nose, and two front paws and say:

"The past has gone,
This is today.
We are one forever,
For that I pray."

Place your cat's front paws over your right shoulder and say:

> *"We are one blessed by love,*
> *Our future is bright.*
> *We are linked from above,*
> *By eternal light day and night."*

Take your cat indoors, play together, and give your familiar lots of attention to bind the pair of you together in love. Snuff out the candle and take your cat to bed with you.

Scorpio Cat

- **October 24–November 21**
- **Key phrase: As your familiar, I think I am the boss.**
- **Stone or collar color: Bloodstone.**

Scorpio cats are secretive and more than likely of a solid, muscular build. They are a perfect witch's familiar because they have an uncanny talent to manipulate people as if they have bewitched them. This magical ability lies in their highly perceptive and intuitive personality. If you feel that a Scorpio cat can read your mind, or put thoughts into your mind, you are right.

Scorpio familiars are passionate, purposeful, and uncompromising. If they share their home with other cats, they will want to dominate. Your complete devotion is what a Scorpio familiar will demand and enjoys most of all.

Scorpio cats do not take chances; they are sensible and not aggressive. They have a sense of humor and charisma, and are genuine, predictable, and loyal. When your attention is divided, they may show signs of jealousy, disappearing in a sulk when you have company and suddenly reappearing when everyone has left. Or your familiar may stare hypnotically at your guests so that they feel uncomfortable and want to leave.

Scorpio familiars may have a hidden life, such as secretly visiting a neighbor to receive more fuss, attention, and food. When you return from a journey, they will probably turn their back on you in disgust rather than greet you.

Bonding Spell for a Scorpio Familiar

Pluto governs Scorpio and your candle and spell ingredients.

You will need:
- **1 burgundy, dark red, or white candle**
- **A straight pin**
- **A leaf from your garden hedge, a holly leaf, or a red yew berry**
- **A small piece of paper (optional)**
- **A new envelope or handkerchief**

Light the candle. With your cat lying on their back, cross your cat's paws backward and forward three times across their own chest while you look into their eyes. Kiss their head, whiskers, and two front paws, and then kiss the tip of their tail while saying:

"Love is present today, to stay, always and forevermore.
I look into your eyes, so bright, and see the light of love.
I kiss your head, whiskers, ears, and front paw,
Our bond is a sacred kiss sealed by eternal law.
For our future magical tale to tell, I kiss your tail,
Knowing we are here for each undoubtedly without fail."

Using a dressmaking pin, prick holes into the holly or hedge leaf to write the initials of your cat's name and yours. Draw a pinprick heart shape around the initials. You may like to press a small piece of paper, upon which you have written your initials and your cat's initials, into the red berry of a yew tree instead—in this case, you will bury the berry.

Place the leaf in a clean envelope or handkerchief and keep this in your purse or wallet so that wherever you go, your cat in thought goes with you, too. The link of love you share can never be broken by distance or time.

Oracle

Chapter Nine

Using the Good Cat Oracle

How to Consult the Good Cat Oracle

Remove the Good Cat Oracle chart from the envelope found at the end of the book. Unfold the Good Cat Oracle.

Select an image from the top row of different cats, ankh, broom, toad, and lion and remember it.

Choose a question from the questions list on page 111. Remember your question and the question number.

While thinking your question, close your eyes and randomly point to a square on the chart. Open your eyes and note which of the sixteen Egyptian hieroglyphic symbols you are pointing at.

From the image you selected in the top row of various cats, ankh, broom, toad, and lion, use your forefinger to trace down to the row beside your question number.

In the row beside your question number, trace with your forefinger to the left or right of that row to find the identical Egyptian image you previously randomly landed on when you had your eyes closed.

Turn to the page headed by that same Egyptian hieroglyphic image. The answer to your question will be beside the specific cat or the ankh, broom, toad, or lion you selected from the top line as the first step to consulting the Good Cat Oracle.

Another way to consult the Good Cat Oracle, if you'd like to have your familiar more actively involved in your Oracle consultation, is to tuck your cat under one arm. With the opposite hand, gently hold one of your cat's paws. Close your eyes and guide (not drag) their paw randomly across the chart. When your hand and cat's paw come to a natural stop, open your eyes and note which of the Egyptian hieroglyphic symbols their paw has landed on. Afterward, follow the same first consulting method.

Instead, you could gently throw a soft toy belonging to your cat onto the chart and follow the described method to consult the Good Cat Oracle.

Questions for the Good Cat Oracle

1. Will the one I love, love me?
3. Will I fulfill my ambition?
5. Is my future brighter than the present?
7. Will my life become more secure?
9. Will I succeed in my new venture?
11. Will my relationship with (name of person) regain happiness?
13. Will I regain my trust in (name of person)?
15. Will I fall in love?
17. Should I forgive (name of person)?
19. What does the immediate future hold for me?
21. What does (name of person) really think of me?
23. Will the plan I have in mind succeed?
25. Is my partner faithful to me?
27. Will my finances improve?
29. How shall I know that the one I love truly loves me?
31. How will I recognize my soul mate?

The Good Cat Spell Book

Using the Good Cat Oracle

	Yes, because you are working hard to make it so.
	Rest assured that it is so.
	A lot more than at this moment in time. Much happiness lies in store.
	If you are cautious, yes, most definitely. Aim high.
	You are comfortable being your own self with this person. They respect you.
	Helpful, a good listener, as well as lovely to know.
	A chance meeting with someone special; quite separately, expect good money news too.
	When your five senses (what you see, hear, smell, taste, and feel) agree.
	It is part of your destiny. Your life will be full of love.
	Through your own actions and theirs, yes. It will.
	The person will continue to love you in the same way as now. Love will grow.
	It is something that you will not regret, so do.
	Eventually, yes. Don't give up trying.
	Yes. Even slow progress is better than no progress at all.
	To let the person believe that you have, will work greatly to your advantage.
	Yes.

Using the Good Cat Oracle

	Yes, because you will find the necessary guidance and help.
	Reliable and trustworthy. A pleasure to know.
	This person is always dependably there when needed.
	No, you can easily see through them and know what they are up to.
	You will be amazed by how much better. Things are cyclic like the full moon.
	If you concentrate your efforts, it will be.
	Your minds think in the same way. At times you are telepathic.
	They are honest and true.
	Something good that you have not anticipated, and many good surprises.
	It is bound to. Have no fear. Look to the future.
	If you believe in yourself, you will fulfill your desire to succeed.
	Choosing good brings heavenly rewards that will astound you.
	You are wasting your time if you think it will happen.
	Surprisingly, it will occur when you least expect it.
	It is most certainly within your power for it to come to fruition.
	Undoubtedly. Much more so.

The Good Cat Spell Book

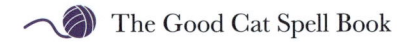

	When you go on a journey, you will. And very exciting it will be too.
	It will most certainly be if you continue to make the right choices.
	With a certain someone, it would be an arduous, worthless, and thankless task.
	Yes. What is ordained to you is wonderful, far greater than your expectations, and definitely well-deserved.
	One day it will just cross your mind and you will know that you know.
	Kind, warm, loving, generous, and wonderful company.
	They say that they are, but are really not.
	A phase of hard work that brings rich rewards in more ways than imaginable.
	This person you are asking about will love you more in the future than at present.
	You will, but it will take time, perhaps longer than you would like. Keep persevering.
	It will make the one in question feel great remorse. That's one of many good reason why to.
	Not immediately, but eventually, yes.
	Not quickly, but steadily. The progress you make will please you and bring the results you want.
	You will, undoubtedly. Strive onward and upward.
	This person will bring out the best in you. And you in them, too.
	You will accomplish good results. Keep confident.

Using the Good Cat Oracle

	Yes, if you put your mind to it, they most certainly will.
	It will make you a better person. You will feel happier for it.
	By feeling complete and fulfilled. It will be like two hearts that beat as one.
	Keep persevering and you will find that it is.
	An invitation to go away for a short vacation. A party invitation too.
	Do not abandon it. You thought of it, so continue.
	As long as you are honest and forgiving, you will. Don't doubt yourself.
	They have your best interests at heart. You are considered in all they do.
	It will happen around a friend's birthday.
	Of course. You probably already know it will, and can help to bring it about.
	You already aware that this person does and will always love you.
	Yes, it is your pre-ordained destiny, written in the stars.
	Not in someone undeserving of it.
	It will fill your heart with happiness. Miracles will occur more than once.
	A good friend who should have been treated better.
	These days, yes.

117

The Good Cat Spell Book

	You will just know it as a feeling when it happens to you. It will be a light-bulb moment.
	Do not doubt, because your luck is ordained in Heaven.
	It cannot be prevented. You can do a lot to make it happen.
	Pretty much, yes. They resist temptation.
	Without a doubt. You can improve on how things are now. A lucky breakthrough is on its way.
	Getting something that you have wanted for a long time. Dreams really can come true.
	With absolute certainty. Rest assured.
	Quite unique and unobtainable.
	Before long, good fortune will bring you great happiness and what you seek.
	There are not too many obstacles, and all are surmountable.
	Do, and you will be appreciated far more than at present. It is a very good idea to.
	The person does and will always love you in a special way.
	You will, but only if you avoid distraction for a while. You possess the powers to.
	You are included in every possible way and constantly in their thoughts.
	Yes, you know within yourself that your mind is set upon it.
	You know how to advantageously endure the betrayal of artificial friends.

Using the Good Cat Oracle

	No one can prevent it.
	Expect fruition soon.
	This person's resignation toward life amuses and strengthens you.
	It will never be the same again. Yes, the potential to is there.
	You share an interest that is your essential nature and theirs. The person's behavior to you proves it.
	In the fullness of time. Keep aiming for your goal.
	They are devoted and trustworthy.
	A new door is about to open into a splendid surprise. You will be utterly amazed.
	Yes, but it will take a great deal of hard work and patience, too. You can do it.
	Many times.
	If you do, you will be respected and appreciated far more than at present.
	Yes, in the way that you wish it to.
	The fulfillment of a much loved desire.
	It is sure to be, so try not to worry. Good luck is on your side.
	In one person, not if you are wise.
	Intelligent, talented, intuitively perceptive, and enlightened.

The Good Cat Spell Book

	Whatever the circumstances, you are always warmly received. Apart from which, you can see it in their eyes.
	You have seen the signs, no?
	If you are sincere and put effort in, of course they will.
	You will feel connected.
	You will feel much better and great relief if you do. So it is a very good idea that you should.
	It is magnificent. Everyone will marvel. Just wait and see.
	Not in a fool.
	If you take positive action and avoid negative thinking.
	Your belief that the person will, confirm your answer is yes.
	You will accomplish your dreams because you are in sync with good. Forces behind the scenes are helping you.
	Far too easily.
	You will if you have confidence in your words and deeds.
	It is right that it should. And it will.
	Strong-willed and obstinate, but very lovable.
	More confidence and self-esteem.
	Yes, of course it will be, and you know it, so stay calm and optimistic.

Using the Good Cat Oracle

	It is not a delusion to think so.
	The damage is done.
	It is within your power to improve matters.
	Too trusting of some people. Very attractive to know and quite mysterious.
	If you devote more of your time to making it that way, yes.
	Hearing from someone you used to know well.
	It will remove hindrances that have blocked your personal happiness.
	Yes, of course.
	You will have no doubt at all if you observe. All the signs are there.
	You have before and you will again.
	If you dedicate yourself to it, you will.
	You already know the answer is yes, so why should you not?
	Your heart would have felt this person's sincere love if it were going to happen.
	Yes, and it will be a blessing too when it does.
	Better than your expectations, most certainly yes.
	There will be no question or doubt about it when that person appears.

121

The Good Cat Spell Book

	It is perfectly within your capabilities to make an upswing happen.
	Do, and then let go of it. Try to not think about it again.
	The person's sincerity will shine through all their actions.
	Not as interested in them as they are in you. They wish it were not that way.
	It is perfectly possible, yes. Aim at your target.
	An achievement beyond your wildest dreams.
	In mind and in body.
	They bring out the best in you and enhance your abilities. Apart from that, your intuition will tell you.
	Wait and see how, most definitely, it is. Many bright, happy times are ahead.
	Rest assured, yes. You are more capable of organizing matters than you perhaps realize.
	With one, most certainly not.
	You know better than to doubt that you will not, because you know that you will.
	Yes, within twelve months.
	If you sincerely want it to, it will. You are in a strong position.
	You will because of your relentless efforts.
	You know in your heart that the person already has loving feelings for you.

Using the Good Cat Oracle

	The present is not as happy as your life will be in the days, months, and years to come.
	Things will be unnecessarily hard if you do not.
	Not at the moment. But given time it will.
	You will feel that you have always known them.
	Better times return soon, yes.
	You are protected by higher forces looking after you, especially your guardian angel.
	Most charming, kind, generous, and spiritually and academically gifted.
	They will want to show you off to their friends and family.
	You should not doubt your abilities to succeed at achieving your potential.
	Try harder and you will be amazed at how and when these matters unfold for you.
	With maybe one or two wrong ones before your intended.
	Yes, do, and continue to again and again.
	You will make sure that they do, that is surely true.
	The appreciation of respected people.
	Yes, they dare not be otherwise. They are aware you can read them like a book.
	Yes, someone will let you know that you are loved.

The Good Cat Spell Book

	Most certainly. Yes.
	They would like to see you more often.
	If you work at it, yes. You have every reason to feel hopeful.
	Yes, for your own peace of mind as well as theirs.
	A reunion that you did not expect to happen.
	They will want to do all they can to make you happy.
	Yes, it will. It is the right time.
	More easily than you presently think, yes.
	With persistent striving and patience, yes.
	Far more than you imagine.
	Certainly, and without a shadow of a doubt. It will be much more.
	You sense that the person will, and you are right.
	It is best that you do.
	It will bring you both happiness and prosperity. Yes.
	It is a spiritual knowing that will make itself felt.
	Sooner than you think.

Using the Good Cat Oracle

	Someone will do a great deal for you for love.
	Yes, truly, because the person likes the feeling.
	In luck, personality, and prosperity, you are better off than the other person.
	They will be good, better than they are now.
	You share the same passion.
	They want it to.
	A better understanding with people of importance and those who love you.
	If you do not hesitate, yes. Feel reassured and strengthened.
	Even though the person may be undeserving, do. Be pleased you are you, not them.
	In thought yes, but not in genuine deed.
	In and out of it.
	If you decide to, then you will, so the choice is yours. If you do not attempt to, you won't.
	If you try to.
	You have nothing to fear and a multitude of near and far happy events awaiting you in the future.
	You are fortunate and will happily attain it after hardship or testing times.
	Quite obviously, yes, and deep inside your heart you know it will be.

The Good Cat Spell Book

	Of course it is. Much good luck and good fortune will bless you.
	Only if you take more control of yourself and the situation.
	Yes, you are deserving of them being that way.
	Yes, do not give up. You are not wasting your time trying.
	They hold you in very high esteem. Value yourself.
	You will know it when you do.
	You will receive a gift and an invitation.
	Their actions speak louder than words.
	You most certainly will if you put your heart and soul into it.
	It will dawn on you after a while when you are in the person's company.
	Yes, it is undoubtedly right.
	If the person were going to, you would know and feel it in your heart by now.
	No, not completely.
	Yes, a helping hand from someone who cares will make certain that it is.
	Yes, but a little more application to overcome hurdles is required by you.
	If you can find it in your heart to, yes, it will.

Using the Good Cat Oracle

	After struggles and persistence, yes. You have set your mind on making things better.
	Your eyes have the same appearance, and your inner voice will tell you.
	Undoubtedly, yes.
	If you do, you will gain enormously and become more mature.
	A better understanding with people you love who also love you. Bonds will be strengthened.
	Yes, because if you cannot agree, you can agree to differ. Laughter lies ahead.
	Yes, and in a way that will surprise you and others who encourage you.
	Yes. You already sense it.
	You deserve someone better. Maybe you underestimate yourself.
	You will achieve what you are aspiring to attain.
	Perhaps you do not realize how fortunate and gifted you are. They love you.
	Not in the one you have in mind. You will probably always be wary.
	You have every reason to feel cheerful because it most certainly will be.
	Especially if you are thorough in every detail.
	The person's behavior will clearly make it evident.
	You are lovable so yes, absolutely.

The Good Cat Spell Book

	This person is honest with you, totally sincere, reliable and trustworthy.
	You deserve it to be, and it will be.
	To a certain extent, yes. But in one aspect, don't do the same thing again.
	An easier, happier, far more sociable time than of late. Someone will give you some very heart-warming news.
	If you put your mind to it, you can make them. The present situation is temporary.
	They are easily led but do have willpower when they think of you.
	Yes, you will have a lot of good fortune by continuing. A happy turn of events is on its way quite soon.
	Fussy and unpredictable in a very attractive way.
	Not as often as others will with you.
	Yes, give it a try.
	Yes, you will be happier if you take a more positive approach.
	Soon, yes. You will receive words of congratulations.
	You must make certain that you, or an expert you know, reads the fine print.
	Yes, their actions already say so. They want to be with you.
	Yes, in the fullness of time and in a most fortuitous way.
	In this person's presence, you are completely at ease. You can talk about whatever you like.

Using the Good Cat Oracle

	Someone puts you first. Their loyalty is unwavering. You are lucky.
	Yes, very much more. You will be elated.
	Yes. Blessings are upon it.
	Yes, but it may not be everlasting.
	Of course you will, because you are prudent and circumspect.
	Yes, they are.
	Not if you continue in one particular activity. But you are easily capable of making things better.
	Good news that sets you on a bright new path to many good events.
	You understand each other's inner heartfelt sentiments.
	With patience, yes. There is no reason on your part why they shouldn't.
	With someone close to your home.
	Not if you have any sense, and you are very sensible.
	If not then, you will carry it around with you as a burden.
	Quirky and cute. Unlike anyone else they have ever met.
	You know that you can do it and should not delay trying.
	Yes, matters will work out better than you think, so have faith.

Index

A

Acorn, 33, 100
Agate, 82
Air, 15–16, 25, 73–74, 82, 103–104
Amethyst, 86
Amulet, 8, 49, 56, 68
Anise, 52–53, 79
Ankh, 37, 109–110
Apep, 8
Apollo, 9
April, 89, 95
Aquamarine, 86
Aquarius, 82, 86–87
Aries, 95–96
Artemis, 9
August, 91, 97
Aura, 76–77

B

Banishing, 26, 48
Basil, 36–37, 72
Bast, 2, 8–9
Bastet, 8
Birds, 12
Bloodstone, 105
Brain, 18, 73, 83
Breath, 28, 102
Buddhists, 12
Burgundy, 106

C

Camphor, 48–49
Cancer, 101, 103
Capricorn, 88, 93–94
Caraway, 83–84
Catnip, 35–36, 47
Chamomile, 38–39
Chrysolite, 91
Claws, 3, 12, 23, 49, 73, 79, 100
Cloves, 28, 40–41
Comfrey, 87–88
Communication, 75, 79
Crimson, 100
Crossroad, 25, 51

Crystal, 56, 59–60
Cup, 87, 101

D

December, 93, 99
Devil, 10
Diamond, 95
Divination, 67–68

E

Ears, 41, 73, 89, 97, 104, 107
Earth, 15, 25, 82, 88
Egypt, 7–9
Egyptian, 2, 7–9, 37–38, 55–56, 67, 109–110
Emerald, 89
Energy, 3, 15, 43, 59, 63, 67, 82, 91, 96

F

February, 86, 101
Fire, 15, 40, 53, 74, 76, 82, 95
Freya, 9
Friends, Friendship, 38, 81, 84
Fur, 3, 9, 11, 16–18, 20, 27–28, 34–35, 38–40, 44–45, 55–56, 59, 72, 79, 83–84, 94–97, 102

G

Garlic, 40–41
Garnet, 93
Gemini, 82–83
God, 3, 8–9, 52, 55
Goddess, 2, 7–9
Gold, 12, 43, 46–47, 49, 76, 83, 97
Gray, 12, 102
Green, 22, 39, 44–45, 49–50, 77

H

Handkerchief, 20, 28–29, 35–36, 38–39, 78, 83–84, 98, 106–107
Happiness, 3–4, 31, 56, 65, 77, 111
Hearth, 8, 53, 99
Heaven, 3–4, 25, 63
Hieroglyphic, 109–110
Holly, 87–88, 106–107
Horus, 9, 55–56
Household, 10, 85, 89, 101

I

Intuition, 2, 4, 31, 82, 99

J

January, 86, 93
July, 97, 103

Index

June, 82, 103
Jupiter, 99–100

K

Kitten, 75, 79, 81, 93, 95–97, 101

L

Lavender, 18, 38–39, 52, 79, 83–84
Lemon, 98
Leo, 95, 97–98
Libra, 82, 84–85
Lily, 104
Lion, 109–110
Lover, 19, 21, 25–29, 72

M

Magic, 1–4, 8, 18, 29, 46, 79, 86, 96, 102
Mercury, 43–44, 82–83, 92
Midnight, 19, 58
Moon, 7, 9, 16, 20–22, 24–26, 44–45, 48–49, 64–65, 68, 103–104
Moonstone, 103

N

Night, Nighttime, 10–11, 24, 48–49
November, 99, 105

O

Oak, 69, 72, 79, 100
October, 84, 105
Omen, 12, 32, 58, 74
Osiris, 8

P

Paw, 4, 19, 21, 23, 33, 35–36, 39–41, 47, 50, 59–60, 63–64, 69, 73, 82, 98, 100, 104–107, 110
Pear, 85–86
Pebble, 57, 79, 102–103
Peppermint, 79
Pillow, Pillowcase, 20, 28–29, 36, 39, 60, 68–69, 78, 84, 92
Pisces, 101–102
Planet, 16, 21, 40, 43–44, 82–83, 85, 90, 92, 94, 96
Pluto, 106
Poppy, 69
Psychic, 1–4, 11, 67–68, 77, 79, 100–101, 103

R

Ra, 8, 56
Relationship, 20–21, 25–26, 64–65, 84, 87–88, 93, 111

Romance, 15, 18
Rosemary, 79
Roses, 85–86
Ruby, 93, 95

S

Sagittarius, 95, 99–100
Saturn, 94
Scorpio, 101, 105–106
Sea, 11, 24–25, 32
September, 79, 84, 91
Shadow, 1, 22–23
Soul, 4, 8, 21, 23, 31, 63, 82, 111
Stone, 34–35, 56–57, 79, 81–82, 84, 86, 89, 91, 93, 95–97, 99, 101, 103, 105
Strength, 78, 100
Sunlight, 22–23, 34
Sunset, 9
Sunshine, 65, 95, 97
Superstition, 10, 58
Symbol, Symbolism, 8, 21, 37, 46, 56, 109–110

T

Talent, 77, 105
Talisman, 32, 56
Taurus, 88–90
Teeth, 3, 79, 100

Telepathy, 4, 61, 100, 103
Thyme, 79
Tiger, 34–35
Toad, 109–110
Truth, 2, 67
Turquoise, 82, 99

U

Uranus, 87

V

Venus, 16, 21, 85, 90
Vermin, 26, 55
Vet, 57, 59, 104
Vinegar, 62–63
Virgo, 88, 91–92

W

Water, 15–17, 24, 26, 32, 37, 48, 53, 69, 72, 82, 85, 98, 101–103
Wealth, 3, 12, 36, 43, 45–46, 49, 76
Weather, 3, 34, 58, 73–74
Wheat, 32
Whisker, 3, 36–41, 73–75, 100, 107
Wisdom, 11, 15, 67–68
Witch, 10, 75, 105

Y

Yew, 106–107